THE COMEDY OF SURVIVAL

The Comedy of Survival

STUDIES IN LITERARY ECOLOGY

by

JOSEPH W. MEEKER

Athabasca University

CHARLES SCRIBNER'S SONS
New York

Library of Congress Cataloging in Publication Data

Meeker, Joseph W
　The comedy of survival.

　Bibliography: p.
　1.　Human ecology in literature.　　I.　Title.
PN48.M4　　　　809'.9'33　　　　74-1002
ISBN 0-684-13711-9

1　3　5　7　9　11　13　15　17　19　V/C　20　18　16　14　12　10　8　6　4　2

Printed in the United States of America

For Marlene, Ben, and Kurt,
  good companions in the
  scene individable, poem unlimited

Contents

vii

CONTENTS

Foreword

by Konrad Z. Lorenz

A VERY LONG TIME AGO I WROTE AN ARTICLE DRAWING AT-
tention to the fact that certain typical themes keep recurring
as subjects of the literary art of all times and all peoples.
Hymns of praise are sung to faithful friendship, as in the
oldest of all stories ever written, the Gilgamesh epic. The
hero rescuing the damsel in distress is the subject matter
equally of the Scandinavian Eddas and of innumerable
Western thrillers and bad films. The same is true of the
theme of faithful love between men and women, as well as
of some other typical forms of human social behavior. The
opponents of virtuous human beings play an equally indispensable role in all human literature. The villain, in his
most unsophisticated form, appears as a monster of characteristically anthropophagous habits, as the dragon of the
fairy tale, as Polyphemos in the *Odyssey*. Homer, however,
seldom has recourse to villains, for the dangers of the wind

and the sea are sufficent opponents to the hero's achievements; Scylla and Charybdis are demonstrably symbols for purely navigational hazards. Only in more sophisticated literature is the villain represented in human form, with light and shadow used to depict the personality of one and the same human being.

The deep layers of human emotionality contain much that is immeasurably older than humanity itself. Man has arisen from a chain of living creatures which reaches down to the very beginnings of life. His body and his soul are supported and at the same time weighed down by an inheritance which stems from his pre-human, animal ancestors. The evolved "program" of his behavior patterns can be understood only on the basis of its evolutionary history. The English psychologist William McDougall made the daring, though quite correct, assertion that man as a species possesses just as many qualitatively different emotions as he possesses inherited, evolutionarily programmed "instincts." The number of emotions which can stir men's innermost souls is therefore finite. There is a distinctly limited number of socially relevant situations which are able to arouse a specific emotional response.

This explains the otherwise incomprehensible fact that the greatest poets chose for their subject matter exactly the same themes which are consistently used by the cheapest forms of art production, by novelists shamelessly catering to the bad taste of their readers, or by similarly worthless film productions. The hero plays the same role in the Eddas as he does in James Bond novels or in Westerns, and so does the damsel in distress or the faithful friend. This is surprising insofar as one would expect the taste of great poets—of a Goethe, a Shakespeare, or a Schiller—to run along rather different lines from that of highly inartistic producers of trash. However, the amazing identity of subject choice is due to the simple fact that the greatest poets and the most shameless producers of corny literature and films, as well as the most naive among modern consumers of cheap thrillers, color comics, and television plays are all members of the same species and, as such, endowed with the same evolutionally programmed and inherited set of emotions.

There is, however, an essential difference between the manner in which real poets on one hand, and writers of corny novels on the other, produce their works. True art not only appeals to the deep emotional foundations of the human soul, it also originates out of them. The real poet projects into his writing his own basic emotions. He gives utterance to the feelings stirred in his own soul by events and situations which are typically human and which therefore arouse his sympathy. Fear and compassion, by definition the emotions elicited by tragedy, are only special cases of this generally human emotional and innate sympathy.

What characterizes the producer of "commercial corn," be it novels, films, or TV plays, is his lack of such deep emotions. He proceeds much in the manner of the scientific ethologist who, by experimenting with dummies, is able to ascertain those stimulus situations which, in any individual of the species investigated, produce a maximum of the desired reaction. The producer of cheap literature does exactly the same in order to achieve maximum marketability. What is so repulsive and even outright immoral about this procedure is that a product which elicits intense and highly specific emotions in its consumers is achieved, not by the creative genius of an outstanding man who has himself experienced the very same feelings on a higher plane, but by a coldly calculating person who has no human sympathy with the multitude of people who are deeply moved by his work. The danger of this kind of product lies in its coerciveness, which is made possible by the instinctive nature of the elicited response. I myself feel deeply irritated when, while watching the cheapest of corny films or reading a novel by Jacqueline Susann or Victoria Holt, I find myself irresistibly moved to tears. How far more dangerous are literary products which, by the same method, elicit militant enthusiasm and collective aggressivity!

The obvious dangers inherent in the kind of fiction here under discussion are hardly counterbalanced by its one advantage: it can be put to good use by abstracting from its characters those properties which act as "key stimuli" on the readers. In corny novels intended for an audience of frustrated women it is highly instructive to study the properties with which the writer endows the hero in order to elicit the desired responses from the reader. He is always tall and spare, broad-shouldered and loose-limbed, strong and serious, often slightly tragic, and—most importantly—essentially masculine. If the plot of the novel demands some repulsive properties in the hero, the writer may deprive him of an eye or leg or disfigure him with horrible scars but would never dare to make him insignificantly small, fat, pot-bellied, or bow-legged.

If commercially produced pseudo-art can reveal interesting facts about "human nature"—which always means the instinctive nature of humans—real poetry can do the same on an immeasurably more elevated plane. Poetic creation invariably begins with an all-but-miraculous vision, dimly perceived at first and gradually taking shape by a process in which "intuition" plays an indispensable role. The poet is by definition a "seer," a visionary. In the terminology of psychological science, this means a person superlatively gifted with the wonderful, though by no means miraculous, capacities of Gestalt perception and eidetic imagery.

These two capacities reside in the unconscious, yet they compute factual knowledge from innumerable sensory data stored over very long periods of time. From the moment it reaches the level of consciousness, this knowledge appears to the visionary to be quite as convincing as the results of a rational process of deduction. To the genius endowed with this kind of perceptiveness, the truth of what is thus perceived is so obvious that he tends to despise the more pedestrian methods of analytical science. Goethe, perhaps the greatest of visionaries, says: *"Was dir Natur nicht offenbaren mag, das zwingst du ihr nicht ab mit Hebeln und mit Schrauben* [That which nature does not intend to reveal cannot be forced from her by means of levers and screws]." It is obvious that Goethe, like most of his type, does not realize that his knowledge about some of nature's deepest secrets stems from his own perception. Because the processes through which he comes by his knowledge are not accessible to his self-observation, he thinks that his inspiration comes from without. The ancient Greeks assumed the existence of nine Muses, inspiring all artists.

Some of the deep secrets of nature which, at the present state of scientific knowledge, are still inaccessible to reason and analytical thought are clearly revealed to some of the greatest poets by the wonderful though not supernatural cognitive acts performed by Gestalt perception and eidetic imagery. As these cognitive acts are not rational but are rooted in the unconscious and emotional depths of the human personality, it seems only natural that other processes going on in the same deep strata should be particularly accessible to them. The direct understanding reaching out from the unconscious depths of one person to those of another is called "empathy."

Though unconscious and inaccessible to self-observation and reason, the processes here under discussion are no less acts of true cognition than are conscious reasoning and scientific analysis. This fact is borne out, in the most instructive manner, by the few cases in which modern analytical psychology has progressed to the point at which it has become able to check some of the deep truths revealed to the visionary poets of long ago. At this very point, it becomes possible and legitimate to interpret the revelations granted to great poets as sources of scientific information.

This has already been attempted by psychoanalysts, particularly by Sigmund Freud himself. Now, in this book, Joseph Meeker undertakes to do the same, but from different viewpoints: those of literary criticism and biology in general, and of ecology and ethology in particular. On the basis of an impressive overall knowledge of world literature and a good working knowledge in the biological fields just mentioned, he endeavors to interpret the visionary knowledge of the greatest poets of all times for their contents of knowledge of "human nature" in its ecological, ethological, and esthetic aspects. Dauntlessly, he does not hesitate to tackle the most difficult, most ambitious, and at the same time most important question which the ethologist can ask: Which parts and patterns of human behavior are genetically inherited and which are determined by cultural, traditional norms of social behavior? He arrives at some amazing and yet amazingly convincing answers.

His most important discoveries, in my opinion, concern

the widely spread cultural ideology which has contributed to our contemporary ecological crisis. The tragic view of life, embodied in the hero of the Greek tragedy, is based on the deep conviction that man has no part of nature, that he is not subject to natural laws but, quite on the contrary, to a set of emphatically extra-natural or preternatural laws, to moral laws to which his behavior must unconditionally conform. The fundamental theme of all literary tragedy is given by the conflict between moral and natural laws. In the attempt to conform to nature, be it only in the forgivable endeavor to survive, the tragic hero cannot avoid breaking moral laws and so incurring a guilt which, according to the precepts of tragedy, must be expiated. Friedrich Schiller has condensed the tragic view of life in the beautiful last line spoken by the chorus in his tragedy *Die Braut von Messina* [*The Bride of Messina*]: "*Das Eine aber seh ich und erkenn' es klar: Das Leben ist der Guter hochstes nicht, der Ubel grobtes aber ist die Schuld* [One thing I see and recognize clearly: Life is not the greatest of all values, but the greatest of all evils is guilt]."

The antithesis of man and nature as polar opposites not only leads to the unavoidable doom of the human hero, but also to that of nature. "The proud visions affirmed by literary tragedy have not led to tragic transcendence, but to ecological catastrophe," writes Dr. Meeker, who shows convincingly that man's spiritual elevation above his natural environment—an essentially tragic assertion—also leads to the exclusive concentration of all his moral obligations on his fellow human beings: no moral or ethical limitations are imposed upon humanity in regard to the ruthless exploitation of all non-human nature. The introductory chorus of Sophocles' *Antigone* offers an impressive example of this attitude. Meeker says: "Like the engineering mentality, the tragic view of life is a unique feature of Western civilization, with no true counterparts in primitive or in Oriental cultures. It was invented by the Greeks and later modified and embellished by Judeo-Christian thinking." The tragic view of man, for all the high opinion it has of mankind and for all the nobility it ascribes to the tragic hero, has led to cultural and biological disaster.

As a biologist, I agree with this. Like the author, I have "a bias in favor of survival." As an ethologist, I concur with his opinion that a morality which encourages man to detach himself from his animal origins and to regard all nature as subject to him does not offer our best hopes for the future. In fact, I regard such a morality as highly dangerous and I have, in my own writings, blamed Platonic idealism for its preponderance in European thought. This, however, does not imply a difference of opinion: Platonic idealism is indubitably one of the foundations of tragic ideology.

Dr. Meeker's central idea is that the comic mode of behavior is a genuine affirmation of instinctive patterns necessary for biological survival. My own observations of animal and human behavior have confirmed this thesis time and again. Destruction of one's enemies and prideful conquest of nature do not give life its deepest meaning. Reconciliation of opposites and adaptation to environment, the essential values which guide comic behavior, are necessary both to biological evolution and to the full expression of mankind's highest talents. Humility before the earth and its processes, the essential message of comedy, is necessary for the survival of our species.

I also agree with another point which Meeker makes, particularly in the chapter "Hamlet and the Animals."

All idealistic philosophy and most of the humanities are agreed on the assumption that everything which is noble and ethical in man derives from his spiritual, distinctly non-animal nature, while everything that is instinctual and inherited from non-human ancestors is automatically regarded as worthless, if not as positively "bestial" and evil. In his analysis of Shakespeare's *Hamlet,* Meeker shows in a most convincing manner how it is the spiritual, traditional, and cultural morality which unambiguously commands Hamlet to commit murder and the purely emotional, instinctive inhibition against killing which puts obstacles into the path of actions demanded by the tradition of tragic heroism. It is an instinctive and by no means specifically human inhibition which causes Hamlet to "speak daggers but use none," thus behaving immeasurably more "humanely" than human morality demanded of him.

These examples are, I think, sufficient to demonstrate the way in which Joseph Meeker endeavors to extract from the work of great poets their contents of deep wisdom, of unerring though unconscious knowledge about human nature. Some daring assumptions and some sweeping generalizations had to be made in this endeavor. As the author himself says, "A hopeless attempt to see things whole is at least as worthy as the equally hopeless task of isolating fragments for intensive study—*and much more interesting*" (italics mine). He may commit some errors in detail, but how could that be otherwise in an undertaking of equal daring and novelty? The basis upon which this enterprise is founded is unquestionably sound. There is no doubt that all great works of art do indeed, as Meeker says, "provide us with knowledge of the world which transcends the experience of any single individual."

Preface

IF THE WORLD IS INTERESTING ONLY BECAUSE OF THE THINGS humans do, then it is not as interesting as it might be. The things of the earth are as provocative and important as the works of art or philosophical systems created by humans, and they can no longer be relegated to scientific laboratories. However exalted one's view of mankind, the time has passed when it was possible to think of the world as man's oyster, or even as his garden. Those who attend exclusively to human affairs will find it increasingly difficult to understand their own experience, to live a rich life, and to survive.

Environmental crisis has become the occasion for a searching reevaluation of human culture and its relationships to natural processes. Degradation of world biological stability is now obvious and threatening. It is not the work of some inhuman technological demon, but a logical consequence of human beliefs and values, human toys and tools, and the use of the world for strictly human satisfaction. Philosophies, religions, and arts which define and express human values also guide the human use and misuse of nature. Human culture and environmental crisis are intimately and causally interrelated.

Although some human beliefs can lead to ecological disruption, as they evidently have done, others may lead toward greater integration of mankind with the natural ecology of the world. This book is an exploration of the possible correspondences between the cultural creations of mankind, especially literature, and the requirements of a balanced natural ecology.

Much that has been loved and admired by a humanistic culture is unfortunately incompatible with biological stability. It is not misanthropic to criticize such noble traditions as literary tragedy and humanism which have flattered the human ego while jeopardizing the survival of our species. Deep admiration for the unique creations of human art and thought justifies my hope that mankind and civilization will persist. That hope, it appears, can be realized only if many other forms of life thrive as well. If cherished human traditions have led to damage of the world, then those traditions must be revised.

There is much within human culture that has encouraged congenial and cooperative integration of humanity with natural environments. It is my purpose to identify some of those patterns within human art and thought which hold most promise for a fully developed human cultural and artistic life consistent with a diverse and stable natural ecology. The way out of environmental crisis does not lead back to the supposed simplicity of the cave or the farm, but toward a more intricate form of living guided by a complex human mind seeking to find its appropriate place upon a complex earth.

Initial studies for this book were supported by a fellowship grant from the National Endowment for the Humanities. Additional friendly help came from Dr. Konrad Lorenz and his wife Gretl, who invited me into their home in Germany for nearly a month's field study and conversation about ethology. Sir Frank Fraser Darling similarly provided hospitality and good advice on relationships between art and ecology. Professors Arne Naess and Eivind Østbye of the University of Oslo offered insight into philosophical problems raised by ecology. Longer-term support and encouragement came from Professors Richard Cooley and Robert Edgar, both of the University of California at Santa Cruz. Many people gave useful criticism and advice, most notably Gregory Bateson, William Berry, Warren Carrier, Donald Elgin, David Klein, Leo Marx, Adolph Murie, Todd Newberry, Paul Shepard, Paul Weiss, and L. T. Yacasua. Secretarial services were provided by Betsy Wootten and Evelyn Day. Robley Wilson and Loree Rackstraw encouraged me and printed portions of the book in the *North American Review*.

THE COMEDY OF SURVIVAL

ONE

An Introduction to Literary Ecology

HUMAN BEINGS ARE THE EARTH'S ONLY LITERARY CREAtures. Lacking the plants' talent for photosynthesis and unable to fly like birds, humans are yet able to write great epic poems and mediocre office memos, thanks to the peculiar development of their brains. It is generally assumed that this unique literary talent bestows upon mankind a special dignity not enjoyed by other animals. Whooping cranes, were they blessed with self-consciousness, might feel the same about their sophisticated mating rituals. Like us, they might translate their specific peculiarities into status symbols affirming their worth in the world. We would laugh at them, for in honest moments we know well enough that uniqueness does not in itself confer superiority.

If the creation of literature is an important characteristic of the human species, it should be examined carefully and honestly to discover its influence upon human behavior and the natural environment—to determine what role, if any, it plays in the welfare and survival of mankind and what insight it offers into human relationships with other species and with the world around us. Is it an activity which adapts us better to the world or one which estranges us from it? From the unforgiving perspective of evolution and natural selection, does literature contribute more to our survival than it does to our extinction? Such questions are perhaps no more answerable than those concerning dignity and status, but they may at least lead to new insight rather than to an increase of the traditional human anthropocentric smugness. This book will explore these questions in search of links between literature and the phenomena of nature.

As an evolutionary experiment, human consciousness and its systems of literary notation are too recent to judge with much confidence. Ten thousand years of accumulated human thought, only some six thousand in written records, constitutes slim evidence for evaluating the importance of an evolutionary innovation. What evidence there is, moreover, seems contradictory or uncertain. The unusual human brain has permitted human adaptation to every known natural environment and the manipulation of those environments where human adaptation is marginal. It has led to the domestication of plants and animals on a large scale, thus allowing for rapid population growth and for the development of cities and civilizations. It has created tools to extend human bodily powers and technologies to organize those tools. It has produced painting, sculpture, music, religion, philosophy, and literature.

The activity of the human brain has also brought about the extinction of many animal species and the wholesale disruption of world ecosystems. It now threatens to destroy most of what it has created and much that it has not.

Considering the novelty of consciousness as an evolution-

4

ary device, one would expect to find many false starts and mistakes in these years of its early development. How many millions of disasters and millions of years were required to develop successful wings for birds or useful protective coloring for small mammals and insects? The human mind deserves at least as much margin for error as these inventions. There is a tendency to be intolerant of its imperfections, to announce the end of everything when problems arise which the human mind cannot immediately solve.

People fret now because a new crisis of consciousness is upon us. It may date from Earth Day in 1970, from the first atomic bomb, from the industrial revolution, from the Renaissance, from the fall of Rome, or from the rise of Greek philosophy in the fifth century B.C. Within the Western tradition, the sense of apocalypse is so old that it seems a permanent and universal feature of the human condition. Whatever its origin, it may be stronger in our time than it has been before. The scientific and psychological signs of imminent catastrophe are abundant and compelling. However we may fish for redemptive schemes or scramble for solutions to avoid destruction, increasing numbers of thinking people expect that people may not be long for this world.

Environmental crisis is the most recent symbol of apocalyptic expectations, and it may be the most pervasive and powerful threat yet recognized. Ecological disaster promises to undermine human life and perhaps the conditions required by all life, not merely this or that political state, ideology, or religious tradition. Its potency is more frightening than that of biblical floods or famines because it is a product of concerted human intentions over the past six thousand years of cultural history. No vengeful deity is punishing mankind for wrongdoing; instead we seem likely to destroy ourselves by succeeding at what was always before thought to be right and good. This monumental irony is harder to bear than mere failure.

Once aware of the powerful ecological image of the end of things, are we yet doomed to live it out? Many optimists recall that people are a problem-solving species which has always risen to its own salvation once a genuine threat has been recognized. Scientists and politicians proclaim their readiness to seek "technological solutions to environmental problems" on the assumption that the same mental inventiveness which has fouled the world can surely tidy it up again. Futurists consult their computers in search of new systems complex enough to accommodate all known needs, human and natural. Conservationists lobby for wilderness protection, better sewage systems, restricted use of agricultural chemicals, returnable bottles. Excellent as such medicines may be, everyone knows in honesty that they treat only the symptoms of environmental disease, not its causes.

The origins of environmental crisis lie deep in human cultural traditions at levels of human mentality which have remained virtually unchanged for several thousand years. The premises upon which our culture has been built are powerful and durable, and their weight upon us must be appreciated before we can hope to alter their structure. Whether they may be subject to modification in the time available is unpredictable because we have so little experience of any such changes in our past. How can our culture change the influence of Homer or Aristotle or Moses or Sophocles upon all that follows from them, including methods of thinking and the inherited images which unconsciously influence human actions? The problem may be of this magnitude. Given such depth, it is possible that "solutions" are more than can be hoped for. Humanity may have to settle for the distinction of being the first species ever to understand the causes of its own extinction. That would be no small accomplishment.

Industry, technology, the exploitation of the earth and the aggrandizement of mankind are governed by ideas, faith, and mythology. The cultural images describing what we might be have helped us to become what we are: however the human mind imagines the world, that is how the world tends to become. If we think of it as a farm, it becomes a farm; if we think of it as a spaceship, it becomes a spaceship, and we can manipulate and direct its circuits toward our chosen goal. We apply human mentality to the earth according to the requirements of the model we have adopted to explain it to ourselves. Consciousness permits the perpetuation of such potent images, transposing them into new contexts and reinterpreting their meaning from generation to generation. That is what a cultural tradition is for, and our institutions exist in order to pass such models along. Education acquaints each new human generation with the models of life and thought available from previous generations. A crisis of consciousness occurs when there is a widespread recognition that many important models of reality inherited from the human past are inadequate, irrelevant, or destructive when applied to present circumstances.

Intentionally or accidentally, literature has been a major source of the models used to perpetuate our past. Writers are only rarely professors or preachers, and few of them seem to expect that their works will be applied to their readers' experience: Goethe was astonished when lovesick young men flocked to commit suicide in imitation of his sorrowful Werther. Some authors have recognized the tendency to imitate literary models and have taken pains to describe its attendant perils: Dante describes the sufferings of Paolo and Francesca who arrived at adultery by reading Arthurian romances, Cervantes attributes Don Quixote's anachronistic career to the reading of books on knight-errantry and Flaubert explains how Madame Bovary's life was ruined by the influence of romantic novels.

Literary success also condemns works of art to inclusion in academic curricula where they become parts of our "cultural heritage." Academic people often see their task in life to be the application of literary and mythological models to the affairs of contemporary life. Like most other readers, they look to literature for guidance in the conduct and interpretation of human affairs. Whatever an artist's intentions may have been, his works are likely to become models, doctrines, or ideologies once they are incorporated into the educational curriculum of a cultural tradition.

Literature expresses deep human needs and represents the forms of behavior peculiar to a consciousness-bearing animal. It is not primarily a medium of communication or and educational instrument for perpetuating certain kinds of behavior but is often treated as if it were both. Because of its relative permanence, literature can be interpreted as if it were a philosophical statement and used as a model to influence the lives of subsequent human generations. Consciously and unconsciously, people imitate literary characters and often try to create in their own lives the circumstances depicted in literature or the motivations which produce its events. Literature which provides models of man's relationships with nature will thus influence both man's perceptions of nature and his responses to it.

8

Ecology is an ancient theme in art and literature, however new it may be as a science. Plants, animals, mountains, seas, and sky have traditionally been represented in literature as a complete system in which human beings find or create their proper places. Major literary works also resemble ecosystems in that they present a large and complicated panorama of experience in which the relations of humans to one another are frequently represented in the context of human relationships to nature and its intricate parts. Imagery describing human life is often drawn from biological sources as people are compared to plants and animals and human characteristics are defined by reference to natural elements. Further, literary works are generally based upon a set of ideological assumptions—usually derived from the artist's contemporary culture, although often in conflict with it—which identify certain principles of nature and define man's relationship to these principles. And perhaps the most pervasive literary theme, running through the literatures of all cultures and periods, is the theme of mankind's role in the structure of the world as a whole. Biological nature is often the image of this larger world.

Literary ecology, then, is the study of biological themes and relationships which appear in literary works. It is simultaneously an attempt to discover what roles have been played by literature in the ecology of the human species. Many academic disciplines must contribute to the study of literary ecology. Literary form must be reconciled if possible with the forms and structures of nature as they are defined by ecological scientists, for both are related to human perceptions of beauty and balance. Characters in literature may also be analyzed as typical or atypical representatives of the human species, and their behavior compared to patterns of behavior among other animals as described by contemporary ethology. Philosophical ideas defining the relationship between man and nature are often expressed or implied in literary works, revealing a history of human beliefs concerning the meaning of natural processes, and also revealing the cultural ideologies which have contributed to our contemporary ecological crisis. Most important, literary ecology makes it possible for us to study the function of literary art as it influences the survival of the human species.

Two relatively new methods of analysis are available for use in such studies: ecology and comparative literature. Both offer techniques of study which have developed over the past century together with the realization that the world is more complicated than has often been supposed in the past. Both are slightly suspect to those who prefer to approach the world as if it consisted of a collection of discrete and separate compartments.

The profound insight at the heart of the science of ecology is that nature is indivisible, and therefore that it cannot be comprehended by studying only its isolated fragments. Ecologists believe that no amount of knowledge of entities will produce understanding of the environment of life unless it is accompanied by an equal understanding of the processes and relationships which bind entities to their circumstances and to one another. Ecologists are therefore interdisciplinary students of nature simply because they have found that nature itself is interdisciplinary. The ecologist must worry about the chemistry of oceans if he hopes to understand the behavior of whales. He must know about the aquatic plants and animals upon which whale life depends, about the economics and psychology of people who slaughter whales, about feminine adornments using perfume and girdle stays, about Japanese dietary habits, and about the mystique of whale hunting embodied in Herman Melville's nineteenth-century American novel *Moby Dick*. All are part of whale ecology, and all must be understood in relation to hydrothermal gradients which influence whale migrations and reproductive behavior, the anatomy and physiology of the whale and its evolutionary history from a land to a sea mammal. Specialists may object that competent knowledge of such diverse subjects is more than can be attained. Ecologists are likely to agree, arguing only that whales cannot be genuinely understood unless such diverse information can somehow be correlated.

Comparative literature is to the humanities what ecology is to the natural sciences. Comparatists examine literary art as a characteristic activity of the human species which is unintelligible apart from its total context of historical and contemporary human life. Here, too, specialists are likely to insist that such difficult studies as philosophy, history, and religion, certainly relevant to literature, require highly disciplined intellectual skills which cannot be mastered together with the discipline of literary analysis. Literary experts have even found it necessary to subdivide their studies into national and linguistic categories, genres, historical periods, and idiosyncratic schools of various kinds, any one of which can occupy the full attention of a scholar throughout his career. There are Milton scholars who have never studied Dante, specialists in Shakespearean tragedy who have only a nodding acquaintance with Sophocles, Ibsen, and Dostoyevsky, and Goethe experts who ignore Goethe's scientific studies and concentrate solely upon his poetry.

11

Comparative literature has developed in the past century among those scholars who have realized that such isolated approaches to literature often distort its meaning.

Comparatists step over academic boundaries because they realize that literature does. Literary artists have never been able to narrow their vision as effectively as literary scholars have. Homer appears to have been as interested in anatomy as in the subtleties of poetic style, Sophocles was as concerned with the psychology of the Oedipus complex as Freud was to be twenty-five centuries later, and Melville was interested in whales apart from their symbolic possibilities. Perhaps it is unreasonable to expect scholars to respond to all such interests among the writers they study. Comparative literature, like ecology, does not insist that it is possible to achieve all the expertise needed for full understanding of its subject, but only that literary study must take into account the intricate relationships found within and among literary works. A hopeless attempt to see things whole is at least as worthy as the equally hopeless task of isolating fragments for intensive study, and much more interesting.

Ecology and comparative literature have flourished in the past half-century together with the dawning realization that human techniques of study should derive their structure from the subject matter which they seek to understand. Academic scholarship has seldom applied this principle in the past, preferring to modify and isolate subjects in order to serve the convenience of scholars. That is one good reason why the academic world has often seemed so far removed from the world of nature and experienced reality. The ivory tower is a place where plants belong in greenhouses, animals in cages, and works of art in drab classrooms. Rats are studied in laboratory mazes and novels in English literature classes. Scholarship and art, science and nature, have thus been widely separated, and the academic world has come to seem less and less like the real world. Both ecology and comparative literature seek to remedy this disastrous separation by assuming that their subject matter itself must dictate the manner in which it must be understood.

The study of process and relationship is an interdisciplinary technique common to ecology and comparative literature. Intensive research into isolated subjects often provides the raw material with which both studies begin their search for overlaps, interdependencies, and common grounds. If the world were schematically represented as an organizational chart, ecologists and comparatists would study the various lines which connect the little boxes, while disciplinary experts would scrupulously examine the contents of each individual box. Comparative studies seek to discover new interconnecting lines which were previously invisible to the experts in their boxes, and so they are sometimes able to add to the contents of the boxes. Ecologists who study food chains, for instance, add new knowledge concerning each species in the chain, and comparatists who study the epic literatures of many cultures contribute to the understanding of every individual work of epic art. Students of process have much to offer disciplinary experts, and much to receive in return.

Experts are masters of the specialized languages of their disciplines, while students of process must often depend upon translations. A humanist who wishes to study the sciences faces something like the task of learning a foreign tongue in order to read an admired author. If it is worthwhile for an English-speaking person to study German in order to read Goethe, Kafka, and Mann, it is at least equally rewarding to study biology in order to understand Darwin, Lorenz, and Ehrlich—and about as difficult, too. No one can learn all of the languages needed for full comprehension of literature or of science. Much comparative work, therefore, must always depend upon "translations." Scientific information must be rendered into a form intelligible to humanists, and literary intricacies must be expressed in terms that will make sense to scientists. Translators of literary works and popularizers of scientific knowledge have always been looked upon with some suspicion, often with scorn, because they fail to reproduce the full integrity of their original material. Robert Ardrey, the contemporary American dramatist and author of popular books about ethology, may represent inadequately the available knowledge of animal behavior, just an Constance Garnett's translations from the Russian may misrepresent the full artistry of Dostoyevsky's novels. Yet for those who cannot learn the necessary languages, there is no alternative but to use the versions that translators and popularizers have made available. Experts often argue that plain ignorance is preferable to such imperfect knowledge. But if a little knowledge is a dangerous thing, it does not therefore follow that it is safe to have none.

Science is popularly thought of as a purely rational quest for new knowledge, while literature is presumed to be an imaginative creation. Scientists are expected to be "objective" in that their conclusions are based on observation rather than on an emotional relationship to the objects of their study. Literary artists, on the other hand, are thought to be "subjective" in the sense that they seek to create and exploit emotional relationships. It is often forgotten that great art is not merely an outpouring of an artist's personal passions, but is a highly disciplined structuring of the concrete elements of experience. It is also true that great scientific work is often expressive of the personality of the scientist. Both contain a strong "objective" element in that they provide us with knowledge of the world which transcends the experience of any single individual, and both are "subjective" in that they include the observer as a significant part of observed reality.

Ecologists, particularly, have found it necessary to modify some of the traditional scientific methods of laboratory analysis in order to comprehend the complexities of natural systems. Zoologists once assumed zoos to be appropriate laboratories for the studies of animals, but no longer. Such important contemporary biologists as the English Jane van Lawick-Goodall and the American George Schaller, for instance, have discovered that ape behavior in the forests of Africa is very different from that seen in the London Zoo, and they have, moreover, found it necessary to *live with apes* in the wild in order to understand them. The noted Austrian ethologist and director of the Max Planck Institute for Behavioral Physiology, Konrad Lorenz, has "become" a greylag goose in his efforts to understand goose behavior. The social activism of those ecologists who participate in the environmental movement depends upon the ecologists' conviction that human beings are inseparable components of natural ecosystems, not merely observers, and that they have an appropriate role to play in the biological environment. Ecology has demonstrated dramatically that science and all human activities are intelligible only as components of larger natural systems, and that humans are part of every system they are capable of observing. Literary artists seem always to have known that.

The Western intellectual tradition has begun to seem

bankrupt to many who have discovered how deep are the lies and distortions it has propagated. Those who despair for the future prospects of the Western value system have a variety of personal options open to them. Some retreat into cynicism or adopt a latter-day version of Roman stoicism, both of which rationalize withdrawal by judging the world to be unworthy of personal commitment. Our culture is also rich in other forms of escape from itself: romantic fantasies, neurosis and insanity, gratuitous violence, and, increasingly, drugs. Another popular—and much more creative—alternative to Western culture has been the study and emulation of Oriental philosophies and religions, where complexity and process are integrated into a vision of life that is less proud but perhaps more honest than the one we have inherited.

However desirable it might be to study Oriental or primitive alternatives to the unsatisfactory heritage of Western culture, it is not really necessary. The Western tradition has provided many value systems capable of guiding human thought and behavior toward more stable integration with natural processes, but these value systems have generally been suppressed or ignored in favor of the humanistic and exploitative promises which have dominated Western culture. Western religions, for instance, have preferred to listen to prophets and doctrines which tell of man's ascendency over nature rather than those which define man and nature as a single integrated system. Westerners have been more receptive to St. Augustine and St. Thomas and Martin Luther than to St. Francis and Dante. Tragic heroism has enjoyed greater respect and influence than the comic tradition. Pastoral longing for a tamed nature has been preferred to picaresque strategies for adaptation and survival under wild conditions. Western science has been regarded as an instrument for manipulating nature rather than as a study which will allow humanity to participate more knowingly in its processes. Anthropocentric humanism has been a stronger force in Western philosophies, laws, and arts than the several available forms of evolutionary naturalism. The majority report of Western civilization has consistently judged mankind to be superior to and separate from nature, and mankind has gladly accepted the flattering implications of that judgment. The minority report, however, has always been present to remind us of our kinship with other animals and our dependence upon nature.

This book is an attempt to read some pages from the minority report, comparing its values and implications with those of the dominant strain of western culture and checking its insights against some of the findings of contemporary biological sciences. The revolution in biological thought which has been begun in this century with such studies as ecology and ethology is in part an affirmation of the minority vision, a vision articulated by a few literary artists and unpopular philosophers but rarely heard by statesmen, religious leaders, or educators. If the new messages of biology can be brought together with the old messages of philosophy and literature, perhaps they may become a unified statement in the minds and hearts of the people who will assume leadership tomorrow.

Literature, like science, has as often contributed to the destruction or degradation of biological environments as to their greater health and stability. Both are features of the natural history of our species, capable of adapting us better to the world or of estranging us further from it. The studies which follow are an attempt to identify some adaptive and maladaptive postures in the literary traditions of human culture and to enlist support for those which offer the prospect of a human future in closer agreement with the processes of nature than much of the human past has been.

TWO

The Comic Mode

THE BIOLOGY OF COMEDY

LITERARY CRITICISM HAS ASSERTED FROM ITS BEGINNINGS THE idea that literature is essentially an imitation of the actions of men. Few have disputed the doctrine of mimesis first spelled out in ancient Greece in Plato's *Republic* and revised in Aristotle's *Poetics,* though subsequent critics have modified the interpretation of the term *mimesis.* Without going into the niceties of the argument, let me merely assume in a simpleminded way that literature does imitate human actions, and consider two examples of such imitation. Both seek to reproduce the same fictional action, but from different historical perspectives and using different literary modes.

The first example is *Oedipus the King,* written in the fifth century B.C. by the Greek dramatist Sophocles. Early in the play Teiresias, the blind seer, confronts the king with the suggestion that the murderer he is seeking is perhaps Oedipus himself.

19

TEIRESIAS
    I say you are the murderer of the king
    whose murderer you seek.
OEDIPUS
                                Not twice you shall
    say calumnies like this and stay unpunished.
TEIRESIAS
    Shall I say more to tempt your anger more?
OEDIPUS
    As much as you desire; it will be said
    in vain.
TEIRESIAS
                            I say that with those you love best
    you live in foulest shame unconsciously
    and do not see where you are in calamity.
OEDIPUS
    Do you imagine you can always talk
    like this, and live to laugh at it hereafter?
TEIRESIAS
    Yes, if the truth has anything of strength.[1]

In *Giles Goat-Boy,* a novel by the contemporary American novelist John Barth, a central chapter is devoted to the translation of the Oedipus story into the idiom of comedy in a post-Freudian world. Barth's version follows Sophocles' closely, but with rather different effect. The Barth account of the meeting between Gynander (Teiresias) and Taliped Decanus (Oedipus) shows all the solemnity of a vaudeville routine.

GYNANDER
        When this play's over you'll
    regret you made that silly vow of yours.
    You tragic-hero types are bloody bores.
                                . . . You're
    the wretch you want. You'll see, when
        Scene Four's done

that you're your daughter's brother,
    your own stepson
and foster-father, uncle to your cousin,
your brother-in-law's nephew, and (as
    if that wasn't
enough) a parricide—and a matriphile!
Bye-bye now Taliped. You call *me* vile,
But your two crimes will have us all
    upchucking:
father-murdering and mother—
TALIPED

                          Ducking
out won't save you. You'll hear from me!
GYNANDER
    You killed your daddy!
You shagged your mommy!
                  [He is taken away] [2]

Both scenes are recognizable imitations of the actions of
men, and in this case the action being imitated is the same:
the revelation of Oedipus's crimes. But the purposes, the language, the moods, and the contexts of the two passages could
hardly contrast more than they do. Sophocles and John Barth
are imitating different aspects of human action, and the
difference between them illustrates a basic distinction between the tragic and the comic views of human behavior.
Sophocles' purpose is to imitate man insofar as he is a creature of suffering and greatness; through his characters he
demonstrates the enormous human capacity for creating and
for enduring pain, for following a passion to its ultimate
end, for employing the power of mind and spirit to rise
above the contradictions of matter and circumstance even
though one is destroyed by them. Sophocles imitates man
as a noble creature. Barth imitates man's absurdity. Barth's
version emphasizes the ridiculousness of Oedipus's situation

and suggests that the hero is slightly dense for not avoiding the mess he's made of his life. Barth's image shows man's innate stupidity and ignorance and emphasizes the triviality of human passions by reducing them to the level of street-corner disputes.

The tragic view of man has not often been achieved. Whole cultures have lived and died without producing tragedy or the philosophical views that tragedy depends upon. Both as a literary form and as a philosophical attitude, tragedy seems to have been an invention of Western culture, specifically of the Greeks. It is shared by those traditions influenced by Greek thought, though few of the cultures even in the direct line of that influence have produced a significant tragic literature rivaling that of ancient Greece. The intellectual presuppositions necessary to the creation of tragic literature have not been present in all civilizations. It is conspicuously absent, for instance, in Oriental, Middle Eastern, and primitive cultures. The tragic view assumes that man exists in a state of conflict with powers that are greater than he is. Such forces as nature, the gods, moral law, passionate love, the greatness of ideas and knowledge all seem enormously above mankind and in some way determine his welfare or his suffering. Tragic literature and philosophy, then, undertake to demonstrate that man is equal or superior to his conflict. The tragic man takes his conflict seriously, and feels compelled to affirm his mastery and his greatness in the face of his own destruction. He is a triumphant image of what man can be. Outside of ancient Greece and Elizabethan England, few playwrights have been able to produce this image in a convincing manner.

Comedy, on the other hand, is very nearly universal. Comic literature appears wherever human culture exists, and often where it doesn't. Comedy can be universal largely because it depends less upon particular ideologies or metaphysical systems than tragedy does. Rather, comedy grows from the biological circumstances of life. It is unconcerned with cultural systems of morality. As the contemporary American philosopher Susanne Langer has put it, comedy is truly amoral in that it has, literally, "no use" for morality —that is, moral insights play no significant role in the comic experience.[3] Similarly, comedy avoids strong emotions. Passionate love, hate, or patriotism generally appear ridiculous in a comic context, for comedy creates a psychological mood which is incompatible with deep emotions. Great ideas and ideals fare no better at the hands of comedy, which ordinarily treats them as if they were insignificant. When noble idealism does appear in comedy, its vehicle is commonly a Tartuffe (as in Moliere's *Tartuffe: or the Imposter*) or a Malvolio (as in Shakespeare's *Twelfth Night*), whose nobility turns out to be merely a sham to conceal selfish or ignoble motives. The comic view of man demonstrates that men behave irrationally, committing follies which reveal their essential ignorance and ridiculousness in relation to civilized systems of ethical and social behavior. As Aristotle puts it, comedy imitates the actions of men who are subnormal or inferior to the social norm and tragedy imitates the actions of superior men.

It could thus be argued that comedy is basically pessimistic and tragedy basically optimistic, as tragedy shows man's potential strength and greatness. This is true only if it is assumed that the metaphysical morality that encourages man to rise above his natural environment and his animal origins is mankind's best hope for the future. That assumption is seriously in doubt in our time. There are good reasons to suspect the wisdom of the traditions of metaphysical idealism. Philosophy since Nietzsche has demonstrated the poverty of humanistic idealism, evolutionary biology has demonstrated the animality of mankind, and contemporary psychology has shown that the mind is guided by many forces stronger than great ideas. Political philosophies fail daily to meet mankind's simplest needs, and now the environmental crisis raises the possibility that the world itself and all its creatures are in jeopardy because humanity has thought too highly of itself. The tragic view of man, for all its flattering optimism, has led to cultural and biological disasters, and it is time to look for alternatives which might encourage better the survival of our own and other species.

Comedy demonstrates that man is durable even though he may be weak, stupid, and undignified. As the tragic hero suffers or dies for his ideals, the comic hero survives without them. At the end of his tale he manages to marry his girl, evade his enemies, slip by the oppressive authorities, avoid drastic punishment, and to stay alive. His victories are all small, but he lives in a world where only small victories are possible. His career demonstrates that weakness is a common condition of mankind that must be lived with, not one worth dying for. Comedy is careless of morality, goodness, truth, beauty, heroism, and all such abstract values men say they live by. Its only concern is to affirm man's capacity for survival and to celebrate the continuity of life itself, despite all moralities. Comedy is a celebration, a ritual renewal of biological welfare as it persists in spite of any reasons there may be for feeling metaphysical despair.

The Greek demigod Comus, whose name was probably the origin of the word comedy, was a god of fertility in a large but unpretentious sense. His concerns included the ordinary sexual fertility of plants, men, and animals, and also the general success of family and community life insofar as these depend upon biological processes. Comus was content to leave matters of great intellectual import to Apollo and gigantic passions to Dionysus while he busied himself with the maintenance of the commonplace conditions that are friendly to life. Maintaining equilibrium among living things, and restoring it once it has been lost, are Comus's special talents, and they are shared by the many comic heroes who follow the god's example.

Literary comedy depicts the loss of equilibrium and its recovery. Wherever the normal processes of life are obstructed unnecessarily, the comic mode seeks to return to normal. The point can be illustrated by a Greek comic drama from the fifth century B.C., Aristophanes' *Lysistrata:* When the young men all disappear from their wives' beds in order to fight a foolish foreign war, the comic heroine Lysistrata calls a sex strike of all women and bargains for an end to the war in exchange for a restoration of normal sexual activities. Lysistrata counts on her own wit and the natural lecherousness of men to solve her immediate problem. Lysistrata's motive is not peace with honor but peace with love—or at least with lovemaking. Honor belongs to the vocabulary of tragedy and warfare. At best it is irrelevant to peace, at worst destructive of it. As Americans have learned during the Vietnam decade, honor can be dangerous and disruptive when used as a principle of public policy. Lysistrata and her women puncture the inflated rhetoric of warriors and politicians to reassert the comic primacy of sex and its attendant social needs: mutual access of men and women to one another, family wholeness, and the maintenance of normal reproduction, child-rearing, and nourishment.

25

Typical of comic action, *Lysistrata* demonstrates no discovery of a new truth and no permanent conquest over an evil force, but merely a return to a former normalcy. No enemy has been destroyed and no new victories have been won. Success is temporary, and it has been accomplished with the most modest of weapons: wit, luck, persuasion, and a bit of fanciful inventiveness. The antagonists are momentarily reconciled, the killing ceases, the men make love to their wives, and the wives raise children and keep house, which is exactly what they were doing before the heroics of warfare interfered with their lives. Like most significant comedy, *Lysistrata* pretends only to show how mankind can hold its own and survive in a world where both real and artificial threats to survival abound. Comedy is concerned with muddling through, not with progress or perfection.

To people disposed in favor of heroism and idealistic ethics, comedy may seem trivial in its insistence that the commonplace is worth maintaining. The comic point of view is that man's high moral ideals and glorified heroic poses are themselves largely based upon fantasy and are likely to lead to misery or death for those who hold them. In the world as revealed by comedy, the important thing is to live and to encourage life even though it is probably meaningless to do so. If the survival of our species is trivial, then so is comedy.

THE COMEDY OF BIOLOGY

If comedy is essentially biological, it is possible that biology is also comic. Some animal ethologists argue that humor is not only a deterrent to aggression, but also an essential ingredient in the formation of intraspecific bonds. It appears to have a phylogenetic basis in many animals as well as in man.[4] Beyond this behavioral level, structures in nature also reveal organizational principles and processes which closely resemble the patterns found in comedy. Productive and stable ecosystems are those which minimize destructive aggression, encourage maximum diversity, and seek to establish equilibrium among their participants—which is essentially what happens in literary comedy. Biological evolution itself shows all the flexibility of comic drama, and little of the monolithic passion peculiar to tragedy.

Ecology is to a large extent the study of plant and animal succession. Ecologists seek to understand the processes through which interactions among species over long periods of time produce the various biological communities and environments found in the natural world. At an early stage in any given environment, pioneering or invading species dominate the scene. These are highly generalized, flexible, and adaptable creatures capable of surviving despite the inhospitable nature of their environments. Pioneers must be aggressive, competitive, and tough. On an evolutionary time scale, their careers are brief but dramatic episodes, but they make possible the more stable ecosystems which follow them. Many weeds that grow on newly cleared land following fires, volcanic eruptions, or construction projects are pioneer plants such as dandelions and crabgrass. Weekend gardeners know well their tenacity and durability. Rats, too, are pioneers capable of thriving against terrible odds by exploiting the meager resources available, as are starlings and several varieties of eels and carp. Many of the species that men find objectionable—the "weeds," "trash fish," and "nuisance" mammals and birds—are pioneering or invading species whose life styles resemble behavior that men have admired most when they have seen it in other men. We celebrate the qualities in human pioneers that we despise in the pioneers of other plant and animal species.

Ecological pioneering species, like human pioneers, are creatures capable of living without some of the normal needs felt by others of their kind. They are heroic individuals who make their homes where no one else wants to live, and their lives lead the way toward challenging and dangerous horizons. They risk death in order to conquer new territory, and their survival depends on their individual qualities of strength, aggressiveness, and often ruthlessness. Pioneer species are the loners of the natural world, the tragic heroes who sacrifice themselves in satisfaction of mysterious inner commands which they alone can hear.

This may sound like anthropomorphism but it is not. I am not suggesting at all that plants and animals possess human qualities but that much elaborate philosophizing about human behavior has been mere rationalization of relatively common natural patterns of behavior which are to be found in many species of plants and animals. The tragic attitude assumes remarkable behavior to be the result of a remarkable personality and an exclusively human prerogative. But Achilles does no more or less for human posterity than a fireweed growing on a glacial moraine does for the plants that will succeed it. The major difference, perhaps, is that the fireweed will indeed be succeeded by different kinds of plants until ultimately a complex forest emerges, while Achilles will be reincarnated by imitators from among his own species for many centuries, to the grief of many Troys and many Hectors.

The process of ecological succession begun by the pioneer

species, if left alone, results in a climax ecosystem. Climax communities of plants and animals are extremely diverse and complicated groupings of living things which exist in a relatively balanced state with one another and with their nonliving environment. A climax ecosystem is much more complicated than any human social organization, if only because it integrates the diverse needs and activities of a very large number of *different* species. Human social systems have only one animal to deal with, man, plus minor adjustments to keep alive the few domesticated plants and animals enslaved to man. But a natural ecosystem accommodates not only the complete life of every species within it, but also provides for relatively harmonious relationships among all its constituent species. In a mature ponderosa pine forest, for instance, thousands of highly specialized types of bacteria maintain stable soil chemistry as each type plays its particular role in the processes of decomposition; insects live upon plants and bacteria and are eaten by birds; small mammals breed in the complex vegetation; larger mammals eat certain specific kinds of plants or prey upon smaller animals; the many highly specialized plants, from small ferns to enormous pines, make up the setting for all other life, provide food and shelter, and in turn depend upon the environmental determinants of weather and geography. It is an unbelievably complicated community in which no individual and no species can survive well unless all other species survive, for all are ultimately dependent upon the completeness of the environment as a whole. The diversity of a climax ecosystem is one of the secrets of its durability.

Life is dangerous for any individual in such a system, for there is always some other individual who needs to eat him. The welfare of individuals is generally subordinated to the welfare of the group. No individuals and no particular species stand out as overwhelmingly dominant, but each performs unique and specialized functions which play a part in the overall stability of the community. It is the community itself that really matters, and it is likely to be an extremely durable community so long as balance is maintained among its many elements.

No human has ever known what it means to live in a climax ecosystem, at least not since the emergence of consciousness which has made us human. We have generally acted the role of the pioneer species, dedicating ourselves to survival through the destruction of all our competitors and to achieving effective dominance over other forms of life. Civilization, at least in the West, has developed as a tragedy does, through the actions of pioneering leaders who break new ground and surmount huge obstacles. Religion and philosophy have usually affirmed the pioneer's faith that only his own kind really counts, and that he has a right —perhaps even an obligation—to destroy or subjugate whatever seems to obstruct his hopes of conquest. Some relatively benevolent societies have provided for wide diversification among men, but none has extended *e pluribus unum* to include other species.

Like comedy, mature ecosystems are cosmopolitan. Whatever life forms may exist seem to have an equal right to existence, and no individual needs, prejudices, or passions give sufficient cause to threaten the welfare of the ecosystem structure as a whole. Necessity, of course, is real. All must eat and in turn be eaten, storms must come and go, and injustices must occur when so many rightful claimants contend. But that is just the point: comedy and ecology are systems designed to accommodate necessity and to encourage acceptance of it, while tragedy is concerned with avoiding or transcending the necessary in order to accomplish the impossible.

One of the tenets of the humanistic tradition is that human beings should try to accomplish whatever the human mind can imagine. Many of our imaginings have been directed toward making ourselves more perfect. The human brain makes it possible to modify human behavior according to conceptual plans which may or may not agree with established natural processes or with human instinctual needs. Unlike other animals, humans can select from a large number of conceptual possibilities the behavior that they prefer for mating, social organization, aggression and defense, rearing of offspring, and the maintenance of food supply.

The capacity to choose one's behavior includes the possibility of choosing erroneously, and many of the environmental problems facing mankind today seem to be the products of mistaken human choices. But what does "mistaken" mean, and how it is possible to know the difference between ecological wisdom and ecological insanity? It is depressing to realize that such questions have been asked seriously only in recent years. Human behavior has generally been guided by presumed metaphysical principles which have neglected to recognize that man is a species of animal whose welfare depends upon successful integration with the plants, animals, and land that make up his environment.

Because they do not have such a wide choice, other animals have more successfully maintained the behavioral patterns which make their own survival possible while contributing to the long-term maintenance of their environments. The recent growth of ethology, the study of animal

31

behavior, is a sign that humans are now beginning to see animals as significant sources of information about living well. Ethologists have consistently discovered that even the simplest of creatures follow exceedingly complicated and often highly sophisticated patterns of behavior, many of which continue to defy human understanding. Animal rituals of reproduction and rearing, defense of territory, maintenance of social systems, nest-building, migrations, and food-gathering are quite as intricate as comparable human activities. The simplest migratory bird has a guidance system that is more subtle and far more reliable than the most sophisticated ICBM, and any pair of whooping cranes has a courtship and sex life at least as complicated as Romeo and Juliet's. We are slowly beginning to realize that we have grossly underestimated the animals.

The truth may be that civilized human life is much simpler than most animal life. We seem to have used our enlarged brain in order to reduce the number of choices facing us, and we have sought the simple way of destroying or ignoring our competition rather than the more demanding task of accommodating ourselves to the forces that surround us. We establish artificial polarities like good and evil, truth and falsehood, pain and pleasure, and demand that a choice be made which will elevate one and destroy the other. We transform complicated wilderness environments into ecologically simple farmlands. We seek unity and we fear diversity. We demand that one species, our own, achieve unchallenged dominance where hundreds of species lived in complex equilibrium before our arrival. In the present environmental dilemma, humanity stands like a pioneer species facing heroically the consequences of its own tragic behavior, with a growing need to learn from the more stable comic heroes of nature, the animals.

Tragedy demands that choices be made among alternatives; comedy assumes that all choice is likely to be in error and that survival depends upon finding accommodations that will permit all parties to endure. Evolution itself is a gigantic comic drama, not the bloody tragic spectacle imagined by the sentimental humanists of early Darwinism. Nature is not "red in tooth and claw" as the nineteenth-century English poet Alfred, Lord Tennyson characterized it, for evolution does not proceed through battles fought among animals to see who is fit enough to survive and who is not. Rather, the evolutionary process is one of adaptation and accommodation, with the various species exploring opportunistically their environments in search of a means to maintain their existence. Like comedy, evolution is a matter of muddling through.

Literary comedy and biological evolution share in common the view that all change is conservative.[5] Organisms and comic heroes change their structure or behavior only in order to preserve an accustomed way of life which has been threatened by changes in the environment. The ancient fish that developed lungs when his home in the sea became untenable was not a radical revolutionary, but a public-spirited preserver of his genetic heritage. The famous peppered moth of Birmingham who changed his color from light gray to black when smoke from the industrial revolution discolored the bark on his native trees may have denied thousands of years of moth tradition, but his adaptation made it possible to preserve moth existence. If there were moral philosophers among the lungfishes and peppered moths, these innovations would very likely have been condemned as threats to the continuity of tradition, or perhaps as shameful immorality. All admiration would no doubt have been reserved for the heroic fish who would rather die than give up his gills and for the moth who nobly faced his end wearing customary gray. Fossilized remains attest to the many extinct animals who insisted upon the propriety of their traditions in the face of a changing world. Of the estimated one billion different species produced so far by evolution, ninety-nine percent have become extinct in such a manner.

To say that change is conservative may confuse anyone who thinks the term is the antonym of liberal and that it describes a mental attitude in favor of traditional social values and customs. The conservative principle in biology is evolutionary; it refers to those variations in structure and behavior which adapt an organism more perfectly to a changing environment, thus conserving its genetic continuity despite changes in form. Whatever may threaten the continuity of life itself is considered by evolution to be expendable and subject to modification, whether it be gills or social rituals. To evolution and to comedy, nothing is sacred but life itself.

The old Italian whoremaster in Joseph Heller's contemporary American novel, *Catch-22*, teaches a similar lesson:

> I was a fascist when Mussolini was on top, and I am an anti-fascist now that he has been deposed. I was fanatically pro-German when the Germans were here to protect us against the Americans, and now that the Americans are here to protect us against the Germans I am fanatically pro-American.[6]

Nately, the naively idealistic American soldier to whom he is talking, sputters in dismay that he is a shameful, unscrupulous opportunist, and the old man replies only: "I am a hundred and seven years old." Young Nately, committed to the idealism of keeping the world safe for democracy, dies in combat before his twentieth birthday. The old man's morality rests upon the comic imperative of preserving life itself at all costs, a principle which overrides all other moral commitments.

Evolution is just such a shameful, unscrupulous, opportunistic comedy, the object of which appears to be the proliferation and preservation of as many life forms as possible without regard for anyone's moral ideas. Successful participants in it are those who remain alive when circumstances change, not those who are best able to destroy competitors and enemies. Its ground rules for participants (including man) are those which also govern literary comedy: organisms must adapt themselves to their circumstances in every possible way, must studiously avoid all-or-nothing choices, must prefer any alternative to death, must accept and encourage maximum diversity, must accommodate themselves to the accidental limitations of birth and environment, and must always prefer love to war—though if warfare is inevitable, it should be prosecuted so as to humble the enemy without destroying him. The events depicted in tragic literature *cannot* occur if these principles are observed. Comic action follows naturally from them.

COMIC SURVIVAL

Oscar Wilde, the nineteenth-century British playwright, offered an important amendment to Aristotle when he observed that life imitates art at least as much as art imitates life. Artists and thinkers, he argued, create images of what life might be like and so provide models for human behavior which men may imitate. Don Quixote was not born a knight-errant, but discovered his profession by reading tales of adventure. People can choose to some extent the roles they wish to play from among the many models preserved by literature and cultural traditions. If people generally see themselves in the tragic mode, it is perhaps because it satisfies their vanity and makes their actions seem important. It is gratifying to think of oneself as a hero, a great sufferer, a martyr, or an oppressed idealist. Oedipus and Hamlet might not have been admired all these centuries if they had not offered illustrious images showing how to bear pain magnificently. But unfortunately, the tragic heroes preserved in literature are the products of metaphysical presuppositions which most people can no longer honestly share, any more than Don Quixote could live up to the requirements of medieval chivalry while living in Renaissance Spain. A post-Freudian world no longer sees incest as an offense against the universe as Oedipus did, nor can we share Hamlet's view that revenge will give peace to the ghost of his slain father. The philosophical props and settings for genuine tragic experience have disappeared. Moderns can only pretend to tragic heroism, and that pretense is painfully hollow and melodramatic in the absence of the beliefs that tragedy depends upon.

Prerequisite to tragedy is the belief that the universe cares about the lives of human beings. There must be a faith that some superior order exists, and that man will be punished if he transgresses against it. It matters little whether this principle takes the form of fate, the gods, or impersonal moral law, for all are symbols of the world's interest in human actions and evidence that the welfare of all creation somehow depends upon what humans do. Corollary to this is the assumption that man is essentially superior to animal, vegetable, and mineral nature and is destined to exercise mastery over all natural processes, including those of his own body. The most respected tragedy further assumes that some truth exists in the universe which is more valuable than life itself. There must be abstract ideas and values which are worth dying and suffering for, otherwise the hero's painful quest for spiritual purity and enlightenment becomes absurd.

"Absurd" is the proper adjective to describe these assumptions, in the rather technical sense in which existential philosophy uses the term. The world has never cared about man, nature has never shown itself to be inferior to humanity, and truth has never been revealed in its awesome majesty except perhaps in the creations of tragic literature. Tragedy does not imitate the conditions of life, but creates artificial conditions which men mimic in their attempts to attain the flattering illusions of dignity and honor. In an age which perceives dignity, honor, truth, law, and the gods as the inventions of egocentric man and not as given facts of the universe, tragedy can only parody itself.

More appropriate to our time are the relatively modest assumptions made by the comic spirit. Man is a part of nature and subject to all natural limitations and flaws. Morality is a matter of getting along with one's fellow creatures as well as possible. All beliefs are provisional, subject to change when they fail to produce harmonious consequences. Life itself is the most important force there is: the proper study of mankind is survival. When the existence of many species, including the human, and the continuity of the biological environment are threatened as they are now, mankind can no longer afford the wasteful and destructive luxuries of a tragic view of life.

As patterns of behavior, both tragedy and comedy are strategies for the resolution of conflicts. From the tragic perspective, the world is a battleground where good and evil, man and nature, truth and falsehood make war, each with the goal of destroying its polar opposite. Warfare is the basic metaphor of tragedy, and its strategy is a battle plan designed to eliminate the enemy. That is why tragedy ends with a funeral or its equivalent. Comic strategy, on the other hand, sees life as a game. Its basic metaphors are sporting events and the courtship of lovers, and its conclusion is generally a wedding rather than a funeral. When faced with polar opposites, the problem of comedy is always how to resolve conflict without destroying the participants. Comedy is the art of accommodation and reconciliation.

Though the comic, ecological view of life may be modest and unheroic, it is anything but simple. Some superrationalists reject the current interest in ecology by arguing that a "return to nature" would be a denial of the mental capacities of mankind, and impossible in a world as complicated and populous as it is today. Their assumption that nature is simple while civilization is complex is one of the sad legacies of romantic thought. Nature is neither an idyll of simplicity and peace populated by noble savages (as pictured by the eighteenth-century French philosopher Jean Jacques Rousseau) nor a bloody battlefield where only the most brutal can survive (as defined by the seventeenth-century British philosopher Thomas Hobbes, and later elaborated by nineteenth-century social Darwinism). Both views drastically oversimplify the intricate processes of nature because they reflect the methods and values of a pioneer species, man, rather than the complexity of the more highly developed species of an ecological climax.

If a "return to nature" were to be based upon the model of a climax ecosystem, civilization would have to become far more complex than anything man has yet produced. Human values could no longer be based on the assumption that man is alone at the center of creation; allowance would have to be made for the welfare of all the plants, animals, and land of the natural environment. Mankind would have to cultivate a new and more elaborate mentality capable of understanding intricate processes without destroying them. Ecology challenges mankind to vigorous complexity, not passive simplicity.

If the lesson of ecology is balance and equilibrium, the lesson of comedy is humility and endurance. The comic mode of human behavior represented in literature is the closest art has come to describing man as an adaptive animal. Comedy illustrates that survival depends upon man's ability to change himself rather than his environment, and upon his ability to accept limitations rather than to curse fate for limiting him. It is a strategy for living which agrees well with the demands of ecological wisdom, and it cannot be ignored as a model for human behavior if man hopes to keep a place for himself among the animals who live according to the comic mode.

When Dante undertook to define man's place in the universe and the conditions contributing to human misery and happiness, the result was a poem called simply the *Comedy*. Dante's poem is perhaps the best illustration that comedy describes a way of life which adapts man to the given biological and cultural circumstances of existence. Dante's comprehensive vision of comic values and behavior will be explored in chapter 8. For now, it is enough to note that Dante's comedy of salvation translates in our time into the comedy of survival.

THREE

Literary Tragedy and Ecological Catastrophe

ARTISTS AND PHILOSOPHERS ARE GENERALLY ASSUMED TO be exempt from ecological guilt. While engineers exploit nature, the poets presumably praise its beauties and the philosophers interpret its moral lessons. Whatever errors may have been committed by means of human technology, the human spiritual tradition is regarded as one that all can take pride in. Plato and Jesus were not environmental exploiters, nor were Sophocles and Shakespeare. On the contrary, the message repeated over and over again by philosophy and literature seems to be that man does not live by bread and bulldozers alone, but must give thought to goodness, truth, and beauty, all of which are ecologically safe.

If it were true that the engineers are environmental villains while humanists are lovers and defenders of nature, Western culture would be even more fragmented than it is. Actually, the engineering mentality has always worked closely with that of the humanists: engineers enthusiastically perform only what the philosophers and artists have determined to be valuable and desirable. The humanities have given consistent intellectual support to the environmental exploitation which is the most distinctive product of Western civilization, and they began their work centuries before the engineers became clever enough to think up ways to implement their ideas.

Tragic literature is an appropriate source for information about the humanistic endorsement of ecological error, for tragedy is unusually inclusive of the values of civilization. No other literary form incorporates metaphysical, moral, social, and emotional attitudes in a matrix as tightly unified as tragedy's. None has more clearly expressed human ideals or explored their implications. Tragic literature is a mirror with impeccably sharp resolution and high selectivity. Its image of mankind is a genuine reflection of man's deepest and most significant qualities, but not of all of them. Like other mirrors, tragedy discriminates among available sources of imagery, selectively emphasizing those qualities it was created to display. Tragic writers, like engineers, have consistently chosen to affirm those values which regard the world as mankind's exclusive property.

Tragedy is not synonymous with catastrophe. Newspaper headlines notwithstanding, it is not a tragedy when train wrecks, floods, or earthquakes kill thousands or when an innocent child is run down by an automobile. Such accidents cause pain and death to many who do not deserve to suffer, but they are not tragic. Genuine tragic suffering is a consequence of deliberate choice. Tragic figures bring on their own suffering, for they have taken a course of action which must inevitably lead to their doom, even though they may not have been aware at an early stage of the conse-

41

quences of their choice. They become tragic because they accept responsibility for their actions and face their pain with the full knowledge that they have brought it on themselves. Their courage is admired even while they are pitied for their suffering. Tragedy, unlike catastrophe, is comforting and flattering to man. It presents the world as an ordered place where some kind of justice or morality rules. The universe is shown to care enough about man to punish him when he goes astray, rather like a stern but compassionate judge. And man appears as a worthy object of love, for he has the capacity to grow and to learn, even to the point of transcending many of his own weaknesses and limitations. Tragic man is ennobled by his struggles, and mankind is ennobled through him.

Like the engineering mentality, the tragic view of life is a unique feature of Western civilization with no true counterpart in primitive or Oriental cultures. It was developed by the Greeks and later modified within the context of the Judeo-Christian tradition. Individual elements of the tragic view of life are present in many cultures, but the peculiar conglomeration of ideas and beliefs that constitutes literary tragedy is a distinctive feature of the West. Further, literary tragedy and environmental exploitation in Western culture share many of the same philosophical presuppositions. Neither tragedy nor ecological crisis could have developed as they have without the interweaving of a few basic ideas which have attained in the Western tradition an importance far greater than they carry in other cultures.

Three such ideas will illustrate the point: the assumption that nature exists for the benefit of mankind, the belief that human morality transcends natural limitations, and humanism's insistence upon the supreme importance of the individual personality. All are characteristic beliefs which appear implicitly and explicitly in tragic literature. Tragedy has gradually lost its power as these beliefs have been increasingly doubted or rejected.

Mankind's Very Own Environment

Hebraic and Greek cultures have asserted from their beginnings that nature exists for the benefit of mankind. In the Genesis account of creation, plants and animals are created to be useful to Adam, and the Garden of Eden is supplied as a fit environment to meet human needs. Adam receives "dominion over the fish of the sea, and over the fowl of the air, and over the cattle, and over all the earth, and over every creeping thing that creepeth upon the earth." Whether "dominion" is to be interpreted to mean responsible stewardship or wanton exploitation is an old debate among theologians (lately revived by environmentalists), but at least exploitation is not clearly ruled out. Adam and his progeny have felt themselves licensed to use their dominion to their own advantage, for it is obvious that people are very important and creeping things aren't.

The Greeks saw nature more as a challenge to human ingenuity than as a god-given source of sustenance, but the superior status of man over nature was never doubted. The choral ode from Sophocles' *Antigone* elaborates the theme of human supremacy, emphasizing man's technological superiority over nature and the miracle of human mentality:

> Many the wonders but nothing walks stranger
> than man.
> This thing crosses the sea in winter's storm,
> making his path through the roaring waves.

And she, the greatest of gods, the earth—
ageless she is, and unwearied—he wears her away
as the ploughs go up and down from year to year
and his mules turn up the soil.

Gay nations of birds he snares and leads,
wild beast tribes and the salty brood of the sea,
with the twisted mesh of his nets, this clever man.
He controls with craft the beasts of the open air,
walkers on hills. The horse with his shaggy mane
he holds and harnesses, yoked about the neck
and the strong bull of the mountain.

Language, and thought like the wind
and the feelings that make the town,
he has taught himself, and shelter against the cold,
refuge from rain. He can always help himself.
He faces no future helpless. There's only death
that he cannot find escape from. He has contrived
refuge from illnesses once beyond all cure.

Clever beyond all dreams
the inventive craft that he has
which may drive him one time or another to well or ill.
When he honors the laws of the land and the gods'
    sworn right
high indeed is his city; but stateless the man
who dares to dwell with dishonor.[1]

Though the earth is "the greatest of gods" rather than a
garden created for man's use, yet man is greater still by
virtue of his inventiveness and power. It is no accident that
a rhapsody extolling man's conquests over nature appears
at a crucial point in Greek tragic drama, for man's spiritual
elevation above his natural environment is an essential
tragic assertion. Mankind is here being praised at the ex-
pense of nature, and only man is of interest to the poet.

Though the land is worn away by man's ploughs and the nations of birds presumably lose their gaiety once they are snared, there is no shame but only praise for the clever man who can inflict this damage for his own benefit. Human dignity is assumed to be independent of and superior to nature, though the conquest of nature is a necessary precondition for its realization. Sophocles has here made explicit man's assumed superiority over nature which is an essential feature of the tragic view of life. It is not that the struggle to control nature is itself tragic, for man is said to master his biological problems with relative ease. His real difficulties are social and metaphysical: how to live with the law and what to do about death, and to meet both problems with something called honor.

Honor and dignity, from either the Greek or the Hebrew perspective, depend upon spiritual states which transcend nature. In both cultures ethical laws which derive from metaphysical principles define the proper activities of man. For the Hebrews, obedience to divine law and devotion to God are supernatural allegiances which determine human excellence. For the Greeks, social order and intellectual integrity are the highest values. Both assume the elevation of man above the processes of nature.

Morality Is Unnatural

Corollary to the belief in human supremacy is the assumption of a metaphysical moral order which also transcends nature. Greek and Hebrew sources are again unanimous in this belief, though they vary in its application. Fate, destiny, the will of God, justice, salvation, honor, are just a few of the terms used to identify the nature of universal order. In modern attempts at tragedy order is more likely to be described in social terms. All these concepts share the supposition that the welfare of humanity depends upon man's ability to live up to a preexisting standard of virtuous behavior, and that this standard is essentially supranatural, the product of spiritual, intellectual, or social powers not governed by the processes of nature. Among the Greeks, violation of the moral order leads to tragedy; the Hebrews and Christians regarded such violations as sins leading to damnation.

Only humans can experience tragedy or damnation since the moral order specifically governs human affairs and does not apply to the rest of creation. Dogs may mate with their mothers without encountering the moral problems of Oedipus, lions may walk into traps without pondering the destiny that moved them to do so, and the many nearly extinct species of plants and animals are not questioners of divine justice as Job was when he saw disaster on every hand. We may feel pity for the sufferings of animals if we recognize that their pain resembles ours, but we cannot experience tragic emotions through them (nor, presumably, can they).

Tragedy is more concerned with moral pollution, an exclusively human phenomenon, than with the biologically universal experiences of disaster and pain. Only humans can sin by departing from the moral order, and humans alone can purify themselves by reestablishing their harmony with that order. "Thy people which thou broughtest out of the land of Egypt have corrupted themselves," says the Lord as he delivers the tables of the law into Moses' hands.[2] Better law is the typical Hebrew prescription for the disease of sin. The Ten Commandments undertake to purify the people by a more perfect regulation of their social behavior

46

and by establishing ritual observances which will remind them of their dependence upon divine power. As prophets interpreted moral law for the Hebrews, so tragic dramatists interpreted it for the Greeks. Tragedy is a ritual purification, in Aristotle's term a catharsis, which immerses us in moral corruption in order to free us from it. We see in the tragic hero the consequences of overstepping the boundaries of moral law; in the process the existence and validity of the law itself are demonstrated.

The Greeks were quite as insistent as the Hebrews that moral law originated above and beyond the sphere of natural existence. Plato's analogy of the cave in *The Republic* is intended to demonstrate that men's perceptions are generally false, and that the source of both morality and truth is far removed from mundane experience. Platonic ideas of goodness, truth, and beauty are independent of experience and unalterable by human actions. All humans can do is to discover their existence and contemplate their meaning, which is what Plato recommends as the proper activity of philosophers. Tragic heroes, too, encounter these absolutes when the actions of their lives run contrary to moral law, and they suffer accordingly. Fate, the gods, and moral law are assumed to exist on a plane far removed from natural existence.

The Ego Is All

Though belief in man's superiority over nature and in the existence of absolute moral law were common to Greek and Hebrew cultures, only the Greeks originated genuine tragedy. The unique humanism of the Greeks placed special emphasis on the individual human personality. While the

Hebrews were concerned with the social problems of the chosen people, Greeks tended to focus upon the psychological problems of the chosen individual. The exceptional personality is always at the heart of Greek tragedy, and subsequent literary tragedy as well.

The tragic hero is an isolated man bearing on his private shoulders the moral burdens of all humanity. He takes himself very seriously, and acts upon the assumption that his personal fate is a matter of great consequence to the world in general. Aristotle's "high-minded" man is one who is conscious of his superior power and intellect, generous with his wealth, and confident of his importance. His pride is the proper mean between groveling humility and selfish vanity. Tragic heroes share these qualities but suffer from some flaw which brings about their destruction in a morally instructive way without decreasing our admiration for them. The tragic hero is a remarkable individual deserving of simultaneous admiration and pity. The extraordinary value attached by the Greeks to such individual personalities is one of their more influential contributions to Western tradition. Tragedy is unthinkable without it.

The unique individual is the focal point of all significance in tragic literature. The tragic hero may be a symbolic person like a king in classical tragedy, or a typical member of a social group or a psychological type in realistic tragedy, but it is his unique personality that is the center of tragic action. He must be highly individualized so that the spectator may experience intense empathy and share his suffering even while recognizing that the hero is in many respects different from himself. If he is too generalized, then the focus will shift from character to idea and the result is a problem drama rather than a tragedy. If he is too clearly

48

symbolic of a larger group or of a personality type, the result is allegory or melodrama. The essential tragic character is one whose uniqueness is not diminished by the fact that he is also a representative of mankind. The Greek tragic heroes who embody this delicate balance—such as Achilles, Oedipus, and Orestes—are among the most admired symbols of the Western cultural tradition.

It is important to distinguish between tragic heroes and cultural heroes of the type found in biblical literature and in other ancient mythologies. Culture heroes represent their people and reinforce the will of the gods, and they stand as moral exemplars. Jacob, Joseph, Moses, and the entire array of Old Testament heroes act for their people as a whole. Their personalities are submerged in the larger process of divine destiny in which they merely play their part. They see themselves as instruments in the hands of God performing divinely ordained tasks. Their actions follow what appears to be a universal pattern for culture heroes: departure, initiation, and return bearing a new message of truth for the good of mankind. This is not the pattern of the tragic hero. He does not undertake the quest for a new truth which will benefit his fellow man, but acts in response to personal challenges and ego problems.

Nor is the tragic hero a leader of his nation or culture in the sense that his actions provide a model for others to follow. Rama, the culture hero of the ancient Hindu epic, the *Ramayana,* is clearly an exemplar of the best virtues of his culture, useful for instructing youthful aspirants in the proper methods of heroism and selflessness. The imitation of Rama has occupied Hindus for centuries, much as the imitation of Christ has governed religious and ethical instruction in Christian cultures. But no one would found an educational tradition upon the imitation of such tragic characters as Achilles, Oedipus, Antigone, Hamlet, King Lear, or Willy Loman, partly because they are sinners, but also because their characters are unique and inimitable.

Greek tragedy demonstrates that unique human individuals are capable of experiences that go beyond the capacity of humanity in general; the tragic hero exists as proof of that thesis. Neither the laws of nature nor the laws of men are absolute boundaries to the tragic hero, but are rather challenges which he must test by attempting to transcend them. The suffering which accompanies his struggle or results from it is merely a price that must be paid for his momentary freedom from the restraints accepted by all other creatures.

In his penetrating analysis of Homer's Achilles, Cedric Whitman, an American classical scholar at Harvard University, articulates the proposition which all great tragedy demonstrates: "The highest heroes are . . . men of clarity and purity, who will a good impossible in the world, and eventually achieve it, through suffering, in their own spiritual terms." [3] This aspiration to accomplish the impossible constitutes the uniqueness of the tragic hero and makes him both admirable and terrible. Whitman identifies Homer's Achilles as the first such hero in literature, but adds that "the baffling vision of self-destruction with eternal glory was native to Greek air, and Homer was the first to frame it in the symbols of poetry and canonize it for the succeeding ages of the Hellenic, and especially the Athenian, mind." [4] The Athenian mind built tragic drama on this unprecedented combination of transcendence and annihilation and set a standard which men and writers since have tried to match.

Personal greatness is achieved at the cost of great destruction. The power of Greek tragedy has etched the idea deeply into the Western mind. Though few have the personal attributes of an Achilles, yet it is no great trouble to translate the tragic assumptions into more modest terms in order to enjoy a smaller share: moderate greatness is achieved at the cost of moderate destruction. And it only requires a small adjustment of one's blinders to overlook the fact that the tragic hero destroys mostly himself, though there is some peripheral destruction of others (Troy is sacked, and the kingdoms of Oedipus, Hamlet, and Lear are left in a state of disorder). The true imitation of tragic heroes is difficult, but it is relatively easy to absorb their lesson that any price is justified for the fulfillment of the unique personality.

It must be remembered that tragic heroes themselves do not generally contend against their natural environments, nor are they exploiters of nature. When Achilles battles the River Xanthos or when Lear challenges the thunderstorm, their real enemies are themselves; the elements of nature are merely used by the poets to represent the inner struggles within the character of the hero. Tragedy is ultimately metaphysical, and it is always evident that biological problems of survival and welfare are of small concern. Tragedy is an art form concerned with moral order and the fulfillment of the individual personality, not with the conquest of nature.

Tragic art, together with the humanistic and theological ideologies upon which it rests, describes a world in which the processes of nature are relatively unimportant and always subservient to the spirit of man. Nobility, honor, human dignity, and spiritual purification depend upon supranatural forces, not upon conciliation with nature. The tragic view of life is proud to be unnatural.

The Decline of Tragedy

Students of tragic literature have noted for the past two or three centuries that tragedy appears to be as dead as an art form. Joseph Wood Krutch, the late American literary critic with a naturalist's eye, lamented the passing of this great tradition but noted that its demise was inevitable once the supporting ideology had lost its grip upon the Western mind. Krutch argued that the tragic view of life rests upon a logical error made early in the development of Western thought:

> The Tragic Fallacy depends ultimately upon the assumption which man so readily makes that something outside his own being, some "spirit not himself"—be it God, Nature, or that still vaguer thing called a Moral Order—joins him in the emphasis which he places upon this or that and confirms him in his feeling that his passions and his opinions are important.[5]

Krutch notes that the intellectual history of recent centuries has presented evidence which seems almost unanimously to contradict these tragic assumptions.

The decline of tragic values has proceeded gradually but continuously since the Renaissance. Every major attempt at tragedy since the Elizabethans has revealed a progressive weakening or rejection of the ideological prerequisites to a tragic view of human experience. The three tragic assumptions examined here—the existence of a transcendent moral order, the assumption of human supremacy over nature, and the importance of the unique human individual—have suffered both reasoned contradiction from science and philosophy and the loss of their former power to excite the imagination.

The Naturalization of Mankind and Morality

William Shakespeare, writing in the late sixteenth century, could not permit his characters to assert the superiority of man with anything like the confidence of Sophocles in the fifth century B.C. Shakespeare's Hamlet, musing over the state of man, repeats many of the terms of the choral ode from *Antigone,* but with irony, not as an assertion of obvious truth:

> What a piece of work is a man! How noble in reason! How infinite in faculty! In form and moving how express and admirable! In action how like an angel! In apprehension how like a god! The beauty of the world! The paragon of animals!
>
> (*Hamlet,* act 2, scene 2)

Hamlet is by no means certain that man is the paragon of animals. He is mouthing the humanist platitudes popular among Renaissance writers and epitomized by the fifteenth-century Italian humanist, Pico della Mirandola, in his "Oration on the Dignity of Man" (1486). The context of Hamlet's homily fails to confirm such platitudes. The humanist credo Hamlet has learned in school is no longer adequate to explain his experience. It is one possible view of man, but not the only reasonable one as it was for Sophocles. Similarly, Hamlet and other Elizabethan tragic heroes are uncertain about the existence of a moral order in the universe. "To be or not to be" is a question to be answered according to one's belief or disbelief in a spiritual and moral order which judges the actions of life and punishes or rewards them after death. Hamlet rejects suicide because he is uncertain whether it will make a difference to his soul, not because he is sure that it will.

Both moral order and human supremacy are questionable possibilities to Hamlet and to Shakespeare's contemporaries, but the importance of the unique individual is still an unquestionable truth. Hamlet knows that he, personally, was born to set right what is rotten in Denmark, and he sees throughout the play that his private decisions are all-important. His remarkable personality, compounded of an unusually keen intellect together with his emotional problems as "passion's slave" make Hamlet an object of mystery to the other characters in the play and to the audiences who have studied him for four centuries. The center of the play is the personality of Hamlet. Even though moral order and human supremacy are doubtful, the importance of individual character remains a certainty. Hamlet will be examined more closely in chapter 4.

Morality as Social Behavior

The assumptions of nineteenth-century realistic tragedy reveal a further decay of tragic values. By the time of Henrik Ibsen, the Norwegian dramatist of the nineteenth century and originator of the realistic theater, the belief in a transcendent moral order has all but disappeared. In its place are the secular orders and disorders of social law and custom. Ibsen's master builder seeks to be a hero by constructing homes for people rather than churches for God. He lives in a world that is neither just nor natural, but is instead dominated by outworn social conventions, an exploitative industrial economy, and much personal pettiness. Human beings are shown to suffer or to prosper according to the nature of their relationships with one another and with contemporary society. They are not superior to nature, nor are they judged by the gods. If anything, Ibsen's characters, like many in realistic tragedy, seem to be inferior to the symbols of nature with which they are compared. In addition to Ibsen's wild duck, O'Neill's hairy ape and Chekhov's cherry orchard come to mind.

But though morality is reduced to social questions and man's superiority to nature is ignored or denied, the primacy of character remains as a sufficient foundation for whatever success realistic tragedy can claim. Ibsen's Solness, in *The Master Builder,* explains and justifies his life in terms which would apply equally well to Greek or Elizabethan tragic heroes:

> There are certan special, chosen people who have a gift and power and capacity to *wish* something, *desire* something, *will* something—so insistently and so—so inevitably—that at last it *has* to be theirs.[6]

The remarkable character is crucial to realistic tragedy, for it is all that remains of the classical prerequisites for a tragic view of life.

The development of existential tragedy advances the suppositions of realism and the decline of tragedy one step further. Friedrich Nietzsche's *Übermensch* and his successors are proud to deny metaphysical morality and to proclaim their kinship with the animals as they struggle to transcend traditional concepts of good and evil, but they never deny their own uniqueness. Ivan Karamazov, a central character in Dostoyevsky's nineteenth-century Russian novel *The Brothers Karamazov*, rejects the moral order with his argument that "everything is permitted" in a world where God and immortality have ceased to exist, yet he affirms his own uniqueness by his tragic acceptance of the moral responsibility which God no longer bears. The theme persists in existentialist literature and philosophy as man takes unto himself the burdens which were formerly God's, with the result that the tragic assumption of human uniqueness is considerably magnified, while moral absolutes and superiority to nature have all but disappeared from the tragic consciousness.

The Deflation of the Tragic Ego

The twentieth century has rejected the last essential tenet of tragic belief, the potential transcendence of the individual personality. Contemporary tragicomedy, the theater of the absurd, and the *nouveau roman* constitute the first full-scale abandonment of the tragic view of life since its emergence in ancient Greece. Absurd characters are not allegorical everymen or tragic heroes in the classical sense, but merely commonplace human beings facing ordinary circumstances. Personality will neither save nor damn them, but is itself subordinate to their predicaments. Personality is thus less important than events, and the possibility of conceiving a tragic hero diminishes.

It is not mere chance that the decline of tragedy coincides with major changes in attitudes toward nature over the past four centuries. Tragedy has depended upon philosophical ideas of the relationship between man and nature, both as a metaphysical foundation for tragic views of experience and for metaphorical imagery used to express character and action. The contemporary French novelist Alain Robbe-Grillet points out that our inherited conceptions of nature are "clogged with an anthropomorphic vocabulary" which has long since ceased to be expressive of our beliefs and feelings.[7] He argues therefore that literature must purge itself of the "pananthropic" notion that the entire universe has a special interest in the doings of man. Robbe-Grillet's rejection of the presuppositions of tragedy is sweeping and complete, and it grows directly from his denial of traditional views of nature:

> There is, then, first a rejection of the analogical vocabulary [comparing humans to nature] and of traditional humanism, a rejection at the same time of the idea of tragedy, and of any other notion leading to the belief in a profound, and higher, nature of man or of things (and of the two together), a rejection, finally, of every preestablished order.[8]

Robbe-Grillet's alternative is to describe creatures and things, man included, without pretending that any necessary relationship exists among them. Without that pretense, tragedy is inconceivable.

The growth of scientific views of nature since the Renaissance has eaten away the footings of tragedy, first by demonstrating that nature does not exist for man alone, then by showing that man's life is of no greater implicit significance than that of any other organism. In our time, man has further learned that attempts to exploit an assumed dominion over nature have damaged the environment necessary to life and dimmed the prospects for survival of his own and other species. The proud visions affirmed by literary tragedy have not led to tragic transcendence, but to ecological catastrophe.

Environmental Pathos

It is tempting to see Western man as a collective image of the tragic hero facing the ecological crisis as tragic heroes have faced other crises. Man has sought the good and brought evil upon himself as a consequence of his efforts, just as all tragic heroes have done. The triumph over nature that has been a cultural goal has at last largely been achieved in the technological West, but has brought little genuine satisfaction. There is tragic irony in the fact that man has achieved the long-sought mastery over nature only to find that his very existence depends upon the natural balances which were destroyed in the process. There is, perhaps, some small room for tragic heroism in this predicament, like that of the man who argues that it takes a real hero to live in smog-smothered Los Angeles. But the nobility of the tragic hero is gone, and only his irrationality remains. He is pathetic, not tragic.

Environmental disasters can never be tragic, for they cannot be conceived as the moral error of an individual. Oedipus caused the pollution of Thebes by his sinful murder and marriage, but who causes the pollution of New York? What was rotten in Denmark could be remedied by Hamlet, but who will take responsibility for what is rotten in Chicago? No hero will suffer transcendently for the extermination of hundreds of animal species or for the degradation of the oceans. Environmental guilt is collective, distributed unevenly among the people now living and those who have lived before. Without a personality to focus upon, ecological crisis presents merely a spectacle of catastrophe with none of the redemptive prospects of genuine tragic experience.

58

It cannot be said that the tragic view of life has caused the ecological crisis; more accurately, the tragic tradition in literature and the disastrous misuse of the world's resources both rest upon some of the same philosophical ideas. The assumption of human superiority to the processes of nature has justified human exploitation of nature without regard for the consequences to animals, plants, or the land. Human concern with a supernatural moral order has directed attention away from the natural environment and minimized its importance to human ethical life. Humanistic individualism has encouraged Western man to ignore the multiple dependencies necessary to the sustenance of life. The search for personal identity and self-fulfillment has minimized man's sense of responsibility both to his own species and to the other creatures with whom he shares the earth.

The rejection of the tragic view of life may be necessary in order to end the long and disastrous warfare between mankind and the natural world. Freedom from the need for tragedy is an important precondition for the avoidance of ecological catastrophe.

FOUR

Hamlet
and the Animals

T RAGEDY IS IRONIC, BUT COMEDY IS AMBIGUOUS. WHEN THE polarized conflicts essential to a tragic view of life begin to lose their power, they are replaced by a pluralized perspective which makes all judgments of value uncertain. The gradual decline of a tragic view of the universe has proceeded rapidly since the Renaissance, but it was well under way by the time Shakespeare began writing in the late sixteenth century. In *Hamlet,* tragic modes of behavior and belief exist side by side with the comic, and the hero straddles the uncomfortable space between. Hamlet is almost as uncertain as modern man whether the world that he lives in is a moral universe governed by dependable metaphysical values, or a biological environment which he shares on more or less equal terms with the other animals.

A central feature of the plot of *Hamlet* is the prince's apparent inability to act when action seems clearly to be called for. After meeting with the ghost of his murdered father early in the play, Hamlet knows what must be done and he swears bloody revenge. Impediments appear or are manufactured by Hamlet, however, so that by the middle of the play it appears doubtful if he is ever going to get on with the business. When everyone's patience is thin, Hamlet revives the violent expectations of his audience and his own flagging resolve with his mousetrap: the play within the play designed to illustrate the manner of his father's murder, to gain a telltale response from Claudius, and simultaneously to validate the ghost's story. It works too well, leaving Hamlet with no further excuse for delay and every reason in the world to take his revenge. "Now I could drink hot blood," he proclaims; given the circumstances, it is easy to believe that he means it.

The audience has two more acts to wait, however, with only a minor murder (that of Polonius) to satisfy partially the bloodthirst that has accumulated. Complications appear abundantly to stall the inevitable violent revenge as the action is diverted to focus upon the queen, Polonius, a voyage to England, the death of Ophelia, squabbles with Laertes, and many lesser distractions of the brain.

The first small distraction is one of Hamlet's most inventive and properly admired manipulations. Immediately following the player's scene, when Hamlet is brimming with vengeful intent, his school friends Rosencranz and Guildenstern arrive to ask him to talk to his upset mother. Moments later Polonius enters with the same request. The three message bearers are all allied with the king and so represent the enemy, but all are personally harmless to Hamlet. There is no direct threat in their manner or intentions regarding him. One might expect Hamlet to brush all three aside or ignore them at such a moment—or, alternatively, perhaps to murder them on the spot if he is as worked up as he says he is. Instead, Hamlet attacks them with the weapons he controls best: metaphor, wit, and imagination.

When Guildenstern asks Hamlet to explain his strange behavior of late, Hamlet in turn asks Guildenstern to play a tune on one of the recorders left behind by the actors. Guildenstern confesses that he lacks musical skill, and Hamlet then drives home his point:

> Why, look you now, how unworthy a thing you make of me! You would play upon me, you would seem to know my stops, you would pluck out the heart of my mystery, you would sound me from my lowest note to the top of my compass—and there is much music, excellent voice, in this little organ—yet cannot you make it speak. 'Sblood, do you think I am easier to be played on than a pipe? Call me what instrument you will, though you can fret me, you cannot play upon me.
>
> [3. 2. 347–355] *

Guildenstern is effectively silenced by Hamlet's scorn, and says no more.

Polonius then enters with similar meddling in mind, but he is disarmed when Hamlet plays upon him like a pipe:

> HAMLET: Do you see yonder cloud that's almost in shape of a camel?
> POLONIUS: By the mass, and 'tis like a camel indeed.
> HAMLET: Methinks it is like a weasel.
> POLONIUS: It is backed like a weasel.
> HAMLET: Or like a whale?
> POLONIUS: Very like a whale.
>
> [3. 2. 359–365]

Hamlet manipulates those who would manipulate him, expending his anger through verbal mockery rather than

---

* References to *Hamlet* are to act, scene, and lines in the G. L. Kittredge edition of the play (New York and Boston: Ginn, 1967).

direct aggression. When he is at last alone, he weighs the hatred that is now confirmed within him and decides how to discharge it:

'Tis now the very witching time of night,
When churchyards yawn and Hell itself breathes out
Contagion to this world. Now I could drink hot blood,
And do such bitter business as the day
Would quake to look on. Soft! Now to my mother.
O heart, lose not thy nature, let not ever
The soul of Nero enter this firm bosom.
Let me be cruel, not unnatural.
I will speak daggers to her, but use none.
My tongue and soul in this be hypocrites,
How in my words soever she be shent,
To give them seals never, my soul, consent.

[3. 2. 370–381]

It is a pity that the two crucial words of Hamlet's conclusion, "shent" and "seals," have disappeared from general usage and so are lost upon most modern audiences. To shend is to berate or strongly reprove, and to seal in this case means to fulfill one's words with actions. The "bitter business" and "hot blood" which occupy Hamlet's mind early in the soliloquy have been transformed into nothing more dangerous than sharp language by its end. He will speak daggers but use none, as he has already demonstrated by his treatment of Guildenstern and Polonius. The late Harold Goddard, an American Shakespearean scholar at Swarthmore College, aptly summarized the theme of this sequence of scenes: "Scorn is a diluted form of murder." [1] Hamlet's preferred weapon throughout the remainder of the play is to be the word, not the sword.

63

Redirection of Aggression

Many ethologists would say that Hamlet's verbal assault upon Guildenstern and Polonius is a "redirection" of aggressive impulses through substitution. It seems to be a common feature of social life among animals that the purpose of intraspecific combat is to gain ascendancy over the adversary, not to destroy him. When animals with the capacity to kill members of their own species reach a point in their battles where death would likely ensue shortly, one combatant will frequently turn aside and ferociously attack some nearby harmless object, like a tree or shrub, or in some other way inhibit his killing behavior or expend it harmlessly. "Honor" among animals is apparently often satisfied by the safe discharge of aggression as well as by its more lethal expressions, and the battle will normally end with maximum face-saving and minimum bloodletting. Slaughter is necessary among animals only for nutrition; when status and the maintenance of social order are at stake, shame and ritualized aggression are more useful.

Animals that live by killing seldom kill their own kind, though they may fight with them frequently. Konrad Lorenz asserts that "there is no single organism capable of self-defence, in particular no large carnivore capable of killing large prey, which does not possess a quite particular system of inhibitions . . . preventing the killing of conspecifics." [2] Patterns of interspecific and intraspecific aggressive behavior differ markedly, and appear to be governed by different parts of the brain.[3] The distinction between the two types of aggression is particularly pronounced among animals equipped with an anatomy designed for killing: "Where one species possesses very dangerous weap-

64

ons such as teeth or claws, which could easily kill an opponent if they were used, special inhibiting mechanisms have usually evolved which prevent killing of the species member; often the entire fight has become transformed into a tournament. Only rarely do well-armed animals use their weapons against a conspecific without any inhibition." [4]

It is obviously necessary to the survival of any predatory species that predation not be applied to a conspecific, just as it is necessary that the stomachs of meat-eating animals be protected against self-digestion. The case is rather different among nonpredatory or unarmed animals, most of which seem to lack strong inhibitions against killing conspecifics, but these species are usually incapable of killing under natural circumstances.

Human Substitutes for Murder

It is not necessary to anthropomorphize animals or zoomorphize Hamlet to see a similarity in their use of redirection at a dangerous moment. Certainly many people who are less symbolically human than Hamlet use his technique often. Judges strike the gavel to their benches when they would like to crack the skulls of lawyers and defendants, and wives break glassware rather than their husbands' necks. It takes a very special effort of the mind to pursue a battle where death or serious injury are likely to result. Military men and dedicated partisans have long since perfected the arguments which convince people to stand their ground in the face of death, but it seems clearly to be a form of behavior that is unnatural, since each human generation must afflict it anew upon the next. Given the opportunity, people have always shied away from killing their own kind in spite of all training to the contrary. When one is distinctly trapped, fighting to the death may look as good as dying without a fight, but if an alternative is available the normal human reaction is to grab at it.

It is possible to ask whether Hamlet is a member of a predatory species blessed with instinctual inhibitions against intraspecific murder. Though this debate is hot just now, the appropriate answer appears to be that he is not. Human anatomical equipment is not well designed for killing, and does not seem to be accompanied by strong, genetically controlled patterns of inhibition against attacking conspecifics. We have made up for our shortage of teeth, claws, poisons, horns, and antlers by our technological inventiveness. Our capacity to kill is mostly a cultural invention, not a natural gift, and we lack the instinctual controls over our weapons that other dangerous animals have. Instinct did not prevent Claudius from pouring poison in his brother's ear, and Laertes was instantly ready to shed vengeful blood when he heard that his father Polonius had been slain. Like our weapons, our inhibitory controls depend upon culture more than upon instinct.

Hamlet's inherited cultural morality tells him that murder in his situation is proper and appropriate. Somewhere within him, however, is a force which resists and looks for alternatives. He creates redirections with his mind when his instincts fail to supply them. Hamlet is an anomaly among heroes because of his strong aversion to lethal violence, though his evasive behavior would seem perfectly normal if it were observed in a wolf.

It is true, however, that human aggressive passions are capable of being discharged short of murder. We do have some basic distaste for killing members of our own species,

66

whether its source is genetic or cultural. And harmless or symbolic violence can sometimes release us from the grip of destructive hate, as literary tragedy is thought to do in the Aristotelian theory of catharsis. We seem to share these features with many animals, particularly those complex enough to live a social existence where they must frequently compete with their own kind.

But is it therefore reasonable to conclude that Hamlet's actions following the mousetrap scene are explicable in the same terms as those of a moose who attacks a willow bush rather than another moose? So obvious and simple an explanation would surely have occurred to someone long ago, and the problem of interpreting *Hamlet* need not have filled so many dreary books. There is nothing obvious or simple about either Hamlet or the moose. The mystery lies in the wonder that such a thing as redirected aggression should exist at all. Allowing that it does (and the evidence from ethology is compelling) it remains to consider the further complications arising from the great diversity of its manifestations. Hamlet's verbal murder of his school chum is as far above a wife breaking crockery as the wife is above the moose who suddenly hates willows. All are redirected aggression, and all serve to affirm the value of life above the values of honor and exclusive dominance.

Comic and Tragic Aggression

Seeking substitutes for dangerous aggression is unheroic and anti-tragic. It is a form of action more closely associated with comedy than with tragedy, with the avoidance of suffering rather than with noble acceptance of it. It is the behavior of Falstaff who feigns death rather than risk battle, or of Don Quixote who attacks windmills and sheep as if they were giants and armies, or of Joseph Heller's Yossarian who makes "evasive action" his moral principle of survival when faced with an enemy bent upon destroying him. Comic heroes consistently devote their energies and imaginative resources to finding alternatives to mortal combat, and are characteristically willing to endure humiliation rather than to kill or be killed. Temporary avoidance of death is a basic goal of comic action; the substitution of nonlethal for lethal combat is its technique.

Throughout most of the play, Hamlet tries to find comic resolutions to his problems. This hopeless search largely accounts for his seemingly inappropriate delay in taking revenge. His initial response to the ghost's demand for revenge is to "put an antic disposition on," permitting him to proceed by dissimulation rather than by direct aggressive action. From this point until the final scene of the play, Shakespeare presents a complicated series of scenes of aggression played skillfully by Hamlet on a verbal and symbolic level. The enemy Claudius and his allies—Rosencranz and Guildernstern, Polonius, and Gertrude—are one by one verbally slain. Guildenstern and Polonius feel the sharpness of Hamlet's tongue in act 3, and such scenes recur with these characters at several points in the play. Gertrude is reduced to tears of shame and frustration by her son's lecture on the immorality of her remarriage. The most powerful mock-aggression of all is staged for Claudius in the mousetrap scene, with Hamlet interpreting the action so that the point will not be missed by the king. Of this scene, Goddard has said, "The play is nothing but a contrivance for murder on the mental plane." [5] Even simple Ophelia is symbolically destroyed by her lover ("Get thee to a nunnery") and she never recovers her balance. Hamlet has been filled with aggressive passion by the legacy from his father, and his action throughout the play is a desperate search for means to discharge that aggression by finding substitutes for murder.

Incidental Victims

Hamlet successfully avoids confronting the genuine object of his aggression, Claudius, until the final scene of the play. Meanwhile, his hate proves fatal to others despite his attempts to redirect it. When Rosencranz and Guildenstern are dispatched to escort Hamlet to England where the king has arranged secretly for his execution, Hamlet deftly turns the tables and arranges for his companions to be killed according to the king's plan. Hamlet recognizes that the deaths of Rosencranz and Guildenstern are incidental to the larger conflict between himself and the king:

> 'Tis dangerous when the baser nature comes
> Between the pass and fell incensed points
> Of mighty opposites.
>
> [5. 2. 60–62]

The same explanation fits Polonius and Ophelia, who also die as unintended victims of Hamlet's aggression toward Claudius. Both are relatively innocent observers of the combat between Hamlet and the king, rather like willows smashed at the scene of battle between bull moose. Ophelia's adolescent perplexity becomes insanity and leads to her death as she fails to cope with the bewildering events around her. Her father Polonius, as Gertrude describes him, is a "good old man" despite his habit of meddling in others' affairs. His inappropriate presence in the queen's chambers at the moment when Hamlet's aggressive passion is at its height (immediately following the mousetrap scene), results in his death by reflex action, not by design.

Hamlet kills Polonius without seeing him, and not as a man but as a rat. Had Polonius been visible as a human being instead of hiding furtively behind a curtain, Hamlet would surely have attacked as usual with words rather than with his rapier, constrained by his consistent aversion against intraspecific murder. Hamlet's distraught mind created instantly an image of an animal competitive with man, the rat, which could legitimately be killed.

Pseudospeciation

Hamlet's murder of Polonius has its counterpart in animal behavior in another sense. Behavioral inhibitions which prevent conspecifics from destroying one another occasionally break down. Under abnormal conditions, so far imperfectly understood, lions occasionally treat other lions according to the patterns of predator-prey aggression, and the normal inhibitions against intraspecific murder seem to be temporarily suspended.[6] Similar behavior has been infrequently observed among wolves and other predatory animals, and seems to occur rather more commonly among rats, especially in densely populated circumstances. Erik H. Erikson, psychoanalyst and professor of psychiatry at Harvard University, has named this phenomenon "pseudospeciation," the adoption of interspecific behavioral patterns of aggression inappropriately applied to a conspecific.[7] The clearest examples of pseudospeciation are to be found in the history of human culture, where this remarkable behavior has become institutionalized. Konrad Lorenz remarks that "pseudospeciation has the consequence that one culture does not regard the members of another as really and truly human. This weakens the normal inhibitions to kill conspecifics and is one of the prerequisites of war."[8] Hamlet's cry: "How now! A rat? Dead, for a ducat, dead!" as he kills Polonius is a small but revealing example of the coincidence of pseudospeciation and murder among humans.

Pseudospeciation has a long history as a feature of human culture. An early and compelling example occurs near the end of Homer's *Iliad*, where the heroes Achilles and Hector at last confront one another for battle. Hector has been chased three times around the walls of Troy before he finally confronts Achilles in a last vain attempt to reason with his adversary in a civilized fashion. Achilles' answer is a classic example of the human use of pseudospeciation:

Hektor, argue me no arguments. I cannot forgive you.
As there are no trustworthy oaths between men and lions,
nor wolves and lambs have spirit that can be brought
    into agreement
but forever these hold feelings of hate for each other,
so there can be no love between you and me, nor shall
    there be
oaths between us, but one or the other must fall
    before then
to glut with his blood Ares the god who fights under
    the shield's guard.[9]

Achilles insists that he is a predator and Hector is his prey of another species; therefore, presumably no constraints to aggression can apply. It is a simple logical trick which allows Achilles to ignore the fact that he and his adversary are both

71

men and so at least theoretically subject to "trustworthy oaths" limiting or ritualizing aggression. Wolves, of course, do not treat other wolves as prey, nor do lions prey upon lions; both behave toward their conspecifics in a relatively polite manner compared to their treatment of prey species, except in those rare instances of pseudospeciation when they seem to forget that they are dealing with one of their own kind.

Identifying the enemy as an animal is an ancient technique of murderers and military propagandists. Jews were dogs or swine in Hitler's Germany, Americans are tigers—even if only paper tigers—to many Chinese, the Japanese were snakes during World War II, and Lieutenant Calley looked upon the women and children of My Lai as "so many cattle" as he slaughtered them. The recent identification of police officers with pigs has worked to encourage similar violence. If an appropriate animal species does not seem to fit the enemy, humans have often invented new nonhuman species to disguise their conspecific foes: wop, honky, gook, nigger, spic, and the host of other pejorative names applied to ethnic groups are pseudospecific categories long used to justify violent behavior. The purpose and effect of these inventions is always to deprive the enemy of the rights and protections normally accorded to other beings. Hamlet has plenty of cultural precedent for identifying Polonius as a rat just before killing him.

Conventional Blood Revenge

The tradition of blood revenge advocated by the ghost of Hamlet's father is also a cultural invention, not an instinctual pattern shared alike by men and animals. No counterpart for the long chains of family feuding over many generations described in tragic literature is to be found in animal behavior. Biological instinct does not seem to affirm the biblical pattern of "visiting the iniquity of the fathers upon the children unto the third and fourth generation," nor is there any sign of an animal instinct compelling offspring to avenge the deaths of their parents. Human language and memory alone make it possible to retain and transmit hatreds and fears long after the occasions which produced them have passed.

Hamlet's prolonged inaction is remarkable because it is an implicit rejection of the morally correct norms of his culture which support blood revenge. Shakespeare has provided within the play an example of "proper" (culturally approved) revenge behavior so that we may gauge how far Hamlet's response is from normal. When young Laertes hears that his father has been killed, he promptly collects a band of supporters who proclaim him king, and with this following he bursts into the throne room demanding instant vengeance no matter what the cost:

> I dare damnation. To this point I stand,
> That both the worlds I give to negligence,
> Let come what comes; only I'll be revenged
> Most throughly for my father.
>
> [4. 5. 131–135]

That is the way a hero ought to be, ready to sacrifice his chances at heaven, the welfare of the state, and any lives including his own which may be required by the code of honor. We shall find no parallels to animal behavior in Laertes' action, for it is unknown outside the context of human culture. Though he proves to have little talent for the role of hero, Laertes at least affirms the traditional model of heroic revenge which is typical of his cultural tradition.

By comparison, Hamlet is a poor example of heroic values. In his influential essay on Hamlet included in the novel *Wilhelm Meister's Apprenticeship* (1795), the German poet Johann Wolfgang von Goethe described Hamlet as "a lovely, pure, noble, and most moral nature, without the strength of nerve which forms a hero," and found in his story "the effects of a great action laid upon a soul unfit for the performance of it." [10] Had Hamlet lived up to the heroic expectations of his culture, he would presumably have murdered Claudius as promptly as possible and assumed the throne for himself rather than experimenting with alternatives as he does. Hamlet's reluctance to kill mocks the tragic and heroic ideals of our civilization.

Hamlet's Gamesmanship

Hamlet tries at every opportunity to convert actions into words, violence into argument, murder into a game. He thus reverses the usual processes of human society which generally move in the opposite direction: from word to deed, argument to battle, games to murder. He is a master of redirected aggression, and his success at avoiding serious violence provides much of the substance of the play. In the end, of course, he must fail and the audience must be satisfied, not simply because of the conventions of the theater but because Hamlet's evasive strategy is unintelligible and unacceptable to his fellow humans. It would make immediate sense to most predatory animals and evoke from them a like response, but among men it merely inspires the escalation of violence.

74

While Hamlet manufactures games, his opponents are inventing plans for action. The final scene of the play begins with a duel which Hamlet sees as an athletic contest, but which to Claudius and Laertes is a pretext for murder. Hamlet accepts the challenge to "play with Laertes" in good sporting faith, hoping to win the duel on points: "if not, I will gain nothing but my shame." Life is not at stake so far as Hamlet is concerned, though he does have a vague intuition that this will not be an ordinary game and confesses to Horatio, "thou wouldst not think how ill all's here about my heart." Claudius and Laertes, meanwhile, are preparing for murder and filling the athletic site with instruments of death: an unbated point for Laertes' rapier, poison on the blade, and poison in the wine. In the duel which follows, Hamlet's entire strategy of life as a sophisticated game is pitted against the tradition of life as heroic action, and Hamlet of course loses even though he is a better fencer than Laertes. Hamlet is forced to abandon his animal behavior of redirected violence and to adopt the human pattern of violent heroics which can lead nowhere but to violent death. The final result is the destruction of Denmark's most important people: king, queen, prince, and a courtier.

Social Responses to Aggression

Tragic literature has frequently demonstrated that prevailing cultural traditions are dangerous and destructive to the welfare of the human species. Aeschylus, the Greek dramatist of the fifth century B.C., was as sensitive to the problem as Shakespeare was in the seventeenth. Aeschylus's trilogy, *The Oresteia,* examines the theme of blood revenge

75

in detail, searching desperately for some way to avoid the endless chain of destruction as each new generation of leaders assumes responsibility for avenging the wrongs done to their parents. Thanks to the unique human capacity for preserving information, revenge can become a traditional pattern of cultural behavior for an indefinite period, causing the destruction of society's most valuable leaders.

In the final play of the trilogy, *The Eumenides,* Aeschylus celebrates the Greek invention of distributive justice. Personal blood revenge is replaced by a jury of twelve citizens which acts in the name of society as a whole and decides issues of right and wrong according to the welfare of the people rather than by the relative destructive power of the disputants. Aeschylus presents this advance as a triumph of Greek rationality over primordial instinct (Apollo over the Furies). Had he known what has recently been discovered about aggressive behavior in animals and its systems of control, Aeschylus might well have regarded distributive justice as a victory of animal instinct over a destructive cultural tradition.

A legal trial is a communal form of redirected aggression. In the interest of social welfare and survival, it restricts combat between antagonists to a verbal and symbolic level, and it imposes punishments mostly in the form of humiliations and restrictions to free behavior rather than death or physical injury. The long debate over the appropriateness of the death penalty and other "cruel and unusual" punishments is a legacy of cultural blood revenge which the Greeks thought they had ended some twenty-five centuries ago. Deliberate execution of deviant or dangerous conspecifics for purposes of punishment is unknown in animal behavior.

Animal societies, like some human societies, do occasionally assume group responsibility for preventing battles between strong leaders when a risk of death or serious injury is present. I recently sat on the edge of a Bavarian marsh with Konrad Lorenz watching his flock of some two hundred grey-lag geese when a serious fight broke out between two strong males, Percy and Ado. It was a grudge match, preceded by several months of skirmishing between the two prominent geese, but this time they went too far. With Ado's beak firmly clamped upon Percy's wing, Percy was helplessly receiving terrible blows from his assailant's heavy wings. Percy would not have survived long had he not managed to take sanctuary under the bench upon which Dr. Lorenz and I were seated. The other geese were extremely excited, and several large ganders were preparing to interfere with the fight before Percy had reached our bench. Lorenz explained that he had observed such behavior on several occasions during serious fights between rivals, when "all the courageous ganders converged on the battle and proceeded to beat the fighters until they were separated." Lorenz also added that during such fights, "I have to keep myself in leash; I find it difficult not to interfere." [11] The citizens watching helplessly from the walls of Troy must have felt similarly as Achilles and Hector fought to the death, and the courtiers of Denmark might have tried to save some of their royalty if the final scene of *Hamlet* had not moved so fast. The social impulse to find alternatives to lethal aggression is as strong as the private need, and it is shared by animals and men alike, though men often suppress such impulses as animals cannot.

An Animal with a Mind

Neither Hamlet nor the humanity that he represents is degraded simply by being compared with animals, nor are animals exalted thereby. Hamlet demonstrates, however, how impossible it is to be at the same time both a good man according to the criteria of tragedy, and a good human animal according to the requirements of nature. Even intellectual and imaginative gifts as great as Hamlet's often do not serve the best individual interests or those of the species. Try as we may to use our mental ability to fulfill our comic instincts for survival, we are unlikely to succeed if we remain, like Hamlet, trapped in a cultural tradition which affirms the supremacy of the tragic point of view.

It is important to remember that alternatives do exist within the Western cultural and literary traditions. Hamlet's mode of action is not the only one available. There are others, which make use of the human mind to affirm and to satisfy natural human needs more successfully. These modes will be examined in the remaining chapters.

FIVE

The Pastoral
and the Picaresque

THE WORLD AS THREAT

THE WORLD HAS ALWAYS SEEMED FRIGHTENING TO ITS IN-
habitants. Ours is not the first generation to notice that social and political structures are oppressive, that inherited
moralities are inadequate guides to behavior, that there
are too many people for comfort, that the technologies
which promised to bless us with ease have also debased human life and the natural environment, or that elaborate
military defenses merely increase the chance of dying in
warfare. It is not that the world is itself malevolent or that
the gods are angry, for most contemporary people are well
aware that the threats to human well-being are of their own
making. The urban centers of civilization and the natural
world outside them have both been corrupted by human
hands. Perhaps humanity's most notable influence upon the
world has been to render it more or less uninhabitable.

As humans have invented their unhappiness, so have they
invented means for relief. Since the Renaissance began to

unfold the new doctrines of humanism and technology, Western culture has sought to evade the destructive consequences by using a variety of psychological and intellectual devices. Pastoral and picaresque literature represent two important patterns of response to an unacceptable world. Both terms are commonly applied to conventional literary genres, but both also identify modes of human behavior and systems of human values. Both are currently in use as models for human responses to contemporary social, intellectual, and natural environments. The choice between them is therefore of some importance in considering what to do about the bewildering world we face.

The pastoral tradition is the older of the two, and its historical credentials are impressive. Some find its origins in the Genesis account of the Garden of Eden, where man's proper environment appears as a fertile and pleasant natural setting characterized by peace and innocence. But the Roman poet Virgil of the first century B.C. gets credit for perfecting the literary form of the pastoral poem with its conventions of sylvan glades, peaceful animals, and happy shepherds who live in love and kinship with nature. Virgil's pastoral was revived at the Renaissance and has since been the model for countless literary works and a major influence upon modern attitudes toward both nature and human society.

The picaresque tradition, appropriately, has no such classical pedigree. Scholars bicker over its literary origins, its definition, and the kind of evidence that might be needed to understand it. There is general agreement that the term derives from the Spanish *picaro,* "rogue," and that the genre comprises tales about socially unacceptable people. The first clear example of the form is the anonymous little book

Lazarillo de Tormes, which appeared in Spain in 1554. *Lazarillo* is the story of a young man's adventures as he struggles to survive in a hostile world which seems bent upon destroying him. To endure, he must adapt himself somehow to the given conditions of his environment, however many rules of decorum and ethics must be ignored in the process. The picaresque, at its origins, is a mode of survival against odds in a world that is indifferent or hostile.

Grossly put, escape from the mad world or adaptation to its conditions are the choices offered by the pastoral and picaresque modes. Both presuppose some necessary relationship between man's social and biological environments, but differ in their assessment of that relationship. The pastoral looks longingly at biological nature as an alternative to society, while the picaresque sees society itself as a natural environment—a wilderness. Western man has lived in a perpetual state of social and biological crisis at least since the Renaissance. Perhaps these two literary traditions can help to reveal whether they are in fact two different crises, or only one.

THE PASTORAL FANTASY

The pastoral tradition is rooted in imperial Rome, though it has significant antecedents in Hellenistic Greece and is reinforced by weighty influences from the Hebrew Old Testament. It was Virgil, however, who set the pastoral tone of greatest influence. Virgil's *Eclogues,* published in 37 B.C., reflects the weariness of sensitive Romans to the excesses and injustices of their society and their quest for solace and sense in a rural setting. "Lo, to what wretched

81

pass has civil discord brought us," [1] exclaims Meliboeus in the first *Eclogue*. Expelled from his farm by war and its political aftermath, he laments the future and admires his friend who has managed to retain land to grow old on: "Happy in thy old age, here, amid familiar streams and holy springs thou wilt woo the coolness of the shade." [2] Rural repose is contrasted throughout the *Eclogues* with "the thankless town," the symbol of anxiety and misery. Virgil's pastorals show man being oppressed by society but comforted by nature.

Rome inspired many besides Virgil to seek relief on the farm, and for many of the same reasons which move modern urbanites to take refuge in the country. Romans of the first and second centuries often found in their city the same features which cause New Yorkers and Los Angelenos to dream of pastoral settings. The Roman satirist Decimus Junius Juvenalis, in his *Third Satire* (ca. A.D. 110–130), presents a familiar catalog of urban ills: degrading poverty in the ghettos, high taxes, inflated prices for poor goods and services, corrupt government, crime and vice in the streets, poor schools and wicked professors, pressures of social conformity, traffic congestion, police brutality, and environmental pollution. "Rome, the great sewer" seems to Juvenal beyond redemption, and his only solution is to go back to the farm:

> Tear yourself from the games, and get a
>   place in the country!
> One little Latian town, like Sora, say,
>   or Frusino,
> Offers a choice of homes, at a price you
>   pay here, in one year,
> Renting some hole in the wall. Nice houses,
>   too, with a garden,

Springs bubbling up from the grass, no need
    for windlass or bucket,
Plenty to water your flowers, if they need
    it, without any trouble.
Live there, fond of your hoe, an independent
    producer,
Willing and able to feed a hundred good
    vegetarians.
Isn't it something, to feel, wherever you
    are, how far off,
You are a monarch? At least, lord of a
    single lizard.[3]

Juvenal's rhetoric, like that of contemporary suburban real estate developers, stresses the goodness of life in the country, and the final lines reveal another familiar motivation: it is better to be lord of a single lizard than a victim of urban exploitation. The city degrades man and the country restores his sense of power and dignity; in the city man is controlled, in the country he controls. A rural setting symbolizes both the purity of nature and the power of man, a conjunction whose paradoxes were present two thousand years ago, though not so fully realized as they have been in our time. Juvenal was hardly a pastoral poet, though he did share Virgil's belief that amid flocks and fields, trees and birds one might find both the spiritual peace and the ego satisfaction which were impossible in the city.

The pastoral goal has always been to find in rural nature an alternative to the ills of civilization. With the decline of Rome, pastoral literature and its attitudes became scarce, perhaps for lack of oppressive cities from which escape was needed. But when the cities arose again with the early Renaissance, pastoral values were revived to meet the needs of harried humanists. Both the pastoral literary genre perfected by Virgil and the antiurban conventions of jaded Romans like Juvenal seemed to express perfectly the sentiments of many emerging Renaissance men.

Disease was one of the more dramatic evils of city life in late medieval and Renaissance Europe. Epidemics of black plague were environmental disasters partly attributable to environmental pollution, humanly induced ecological imbalance, and overcrowding in the newly great cities. When the plague struck Florence in 1348, the aristocratic young men and women of Giovanni Boccaccio's collection of tales, the *Decameron,* sought refuge from death and social disruption in a genteel tour of the Italian countryside where they told one another risque stories to pass the time. Though the *Decameron* is not properly a pastoral tale, its framework shows the pastoral motivation to flee from pain to the solace and pleasure of rural life.

Boccaccio's introduction paints a grim picture of the diseased city where "everyone felt doomed and had abandoned his property," where "the authority of human and divine laws almost disappeared," and where "people cared no more for dead men than we care for dead goats." [4] The alternative to all this misery, sought out by Boccaccio's young people, is a rural garden described in traditional pastoral images:

> The sight of this garden, of its beautiful plan, of the plants, and the fountain and the little streams flowing from it, so much pleased the ladies and three young men that they said, if Paradise could be formed on earth, it could be given no other form than that of this garden, nor could any further beauty be added to it. [5]

The young people weave garlands from the garden plants, listen to the twenty different birds who serenade them, and delight in the hundreds of beautiful rabbits, goats, deer, and "many other kinds of harmless animals running about as if they were tame." [6] To the classical image of a domesticated rural landscape composed of beautiful plants and harmless animals, the Renaissance can add the dimension of moral innocence which derives from the biblical Garden of Eden and the medieval view of heaven as a divinely created pastoral scene. To the pastoral eye, society is bewilderingly complicated and dangerous while nature is beautifully simple and congenial.

The pastoral flourishes in times of urban crisis, or in those periods often called decadent, when traditional forms and rituals of society have become inappropriate but continue to hold the allegiance of large numbers of people who can find no alternative. One result is a general sense, especially among privileged and intellectual classes, that the world is unmanageable, unintelligible, and doomed to self-destruction. Those who have the means to escape begin to look for places to hide from the foreseeable apocalypse, either in a new physical setting or in their fantasies. The pastoral tradition provides both.

Rural life seems rational at such times because it is thought to be governed by natural rather than man-made laws. Crops sprout, mature, and are harvested for human sustenance in dependable cycles. Animals graze placidly in their pastures without all the jostling and conflicts generated among civilized men who crowd the marketplaces. And the rustic farmer who supervises nature's nourishing processes appears to be a contributing part of the sensible system around him, unlike his socially alienated urban brother. To a tired and frustrated aristocrat, agriculture is a symbol of tranquility and order, God's image of what life should be like everywhere.

Nostalgia for a lost Golden Age is satisfied in part by the discovery in the present of simplified forms of order in agriculture and gardening. Agriculture becomes symbolic of both structural integrity and moral innocence. Eden, after all, was merely a small farm characterized by abundance, purity, and simplicity until its agrarian tenants noticed the existence of some awkwardly polarized contradictions like good and evil, male and female, obedience and rebellion, and as result were sent off to build cities where such conflicts belong. The pastoral hope is to reclaim that lost simplicity by escaping present complexity, whether its imagery is that of a classical Golden Age, a biblical garden, a rural landscape, a national park, or merely a suburban lawn with its small vegetable and flower garden to represent the good and natural life in contrast to the evils of civilization.

The pastoral impulse is utopian in its assumption that suffering and chaos are unnecessary and that systems which will overcome such ills are possible, indeed natural. Man's unfortunate choice to leave the garden behind was also an abandonment of reason, of common sense, and of orderly administrative structure, but God has generously permitted vestiges of the original plan to persist in the form of farms and gardens which man may imitate in order to regain Eden. If society can only be organized according to the proper principles of organic gardening, peace and stability will surely follow. The utopian vision, like the pastoral, sees nature at work in agriculture and seeks to reproduce the fertility, peacefulness, durability, simplicity, and moral innocence of gardens among the social structures of man.

Ebenezer Howard, the influential nineteenth-century English landscape architect and city planner, built his utopian Garden City upon a pastoral foundation:

The key to the problem how to restore the people to the land—that beautiful land of ours, with its canopy of sky, the air that blows upon it, the sun that warms it, the rain and dew that moisten it—the very embodiment of Divine love for man—is indeed a *Master Key,* for it is the key to a portal through which, even when scarce ajar, will be seen to pour a flood of light on the problems of intemperance, of excessive toil, of restless anxiety, of grinding poverty—the true limits of Governmental interference, ay, and even the relations of man to the Supreme Power.[7]

Howard's alternative to the pain and degradation of city life, like Juvenal's, is the garden. The difference is that Howard wants to rebuild cities to incorporate the virtues of gardens, not merely to escape from the city. Howard has hope for man. He is confident that the influence of the garden upon the city will provide a solution to psychological, social, political, and even theological problems common to urban environments. His utopian impulse seeks relief in a fantasy of future gardens, not merely in a present change of geography or a return to a previous golden-age garden.

The United States may be the world's largest-scale utopian experiment in creating a nation on the model of a pastoral garden. Many of its earliest settlers looked upon the new land as a green refuge from the oppression they had suffered in European cities. The American pastoral ideal has been studied in detail recently by Amherst professor Leo Marx in *The Machine in the Garden* (1964). Professor Marx has traced the pervasive pastoral strain in American thought and has shown the painful contradictions which developed as the American garden was gradually transformed into an industrialized farm, then into a national factory: "Beginning in Jefferson's time, the cardinal image of American aspirations was a rural landscape, a well-ordered green garden magnified to continental size." [8] An agricultural America must be both beautiful and morally pure, for, according to Jefferson, "those who labor in the earth are the chosen people of God . . . whose breasts he has made his peculiar deposit for substantial and genuine virtue." [9] Marx also shows that the snake of industrialism which was to corrupt the garden was also known to Jefferson. Foreign competition and the War of 1812 forced America to abandon its gardening project in order to defend itself. Jefferson knew that the garden would never be the same again: "Our enemy has indeed the consolation of Satan on removing our first parents from Paradise: from a peaceable and agricultural nation, he makes us a military and manufacturing one." [10] With the machine in power the garden is doomed.

Marx's basic thesis is abundantly supported; the conflict between the pastoral garden and the industrial machine is a fundamental polarity of American thought which has tormented Americans from the beginning. As the machine has achieved greater dominance, the American garden has gradually disappeared, and with it American hopes for realizing a pastoral utopia of peace and purity.

Unfortunately, pastoral gardens are generally made by the machines which must eventually destroy them. In order to maintain the human dominance and safety required by pastoral values, it is necessary to assert man's technological advantage over nature. Predatory or dangerous animal competitors must be exterminated or expelled; poisonous, ugly, or inedible plants must be rooted out; land must be cultivated and sown to nourishing crops or used as pasture for fattening man's sources of meat. Whether the machine is the hoe that Juvenal's Roman is so fond of, the rifle and railroad that cleared the prairies of buffalo, or the bull-dozers, aerial sprayers, and irrigation systems of modern farming, the machine is an indispensable part of the pastoral garden, for it alone gives man the power to civilize nature. Gardens are not images of nature, but of the human manipulation of nature.

The pastoral union of mankind with nature resembles also the marriage of man and woman, but only as male chauvinism conceives of marriage. The feminine garden must be subordinated, plowed, and cultivated if it is to provide anxious males with the peace and fertility they so desperately want. Nature is both mother and bride to man, his source of comfort and pleasure. When Ebenezer Howard described his utopian fusion of urban and rural life, the image that best suited his purpose was that of marriage: "As man and woman by their varied gifts and faculties supplement each other, so should town and country." [11] Howard describes the many services provided by the female countryside for the male town, including love, care, fertility, comfort, beauty, and inspiration, then he concludes that "town and country *must be married,* and out of this union will spring a new hope, a new life, a new civilization." [12] The fulfillment of male needs is presumed to be the only reason for either nature or women to exist at all.

Howard assumes that nature and woman must be tamed before they can become gardens and wives. Once domesticated, both can be exploited for man's benefit, worshipped as symbols of beauty, used for pleasure, and retreated to for comfort. Both are resources, commodities provided for man which must be properly managed if their potential is to be realized. Their conquest confirms the masculine ego in its status as lord and master of creation.

When anthropologists talk about "the pastoral age" they are not referring to a poetic period, but to the stage in human evolution when plants and animals were domesticated, thus encouraging permanent settlements and changing man's nutritional relationship to his environment. That kind of pastoralism freed man from the need to hunt and pick berries, and made it possible for him to pay attention to such things as theology, politics, philosophy, art, and science. Pastoral poetry expresses a longing for this early stage of civilization when agriculture had given man leisure and sufficiency, but before the development of elaborate social and political structures. What the pastoral tradition calls "nature" is merely simplified civilization. No pastoral poet ever gets nostalgic thinking about man as a Paleolithic hunter or australopithecine ape, nor does he care for unimproved wilderness landscapes or violent aspects of natural processes.

The pastoral symphony is a thoroughly domesticated score orchestrated solely around human themes. Its central images—farm, garden, pasture—show nature at the service of man the farmer and husbandman. Pastoral scenes include plants valuable to man for their nutritional or ornamental qualities and animals which have been tamed by man for his own use, such as sheep, cattle, and dogs. The only wild animals are noncompetitors of man, like song birds whose music is assumed to be designed for human entertainment. Dangerous or competitive plants and animals are strictly excluded. The pastoral landscape does not permit thistles or loco weed, wolves, lions, eagles, vultures, mosquitos, or poisonous spiders. And when a snake appears in such a garden, it is a sign that the place has been corrupted already. Pastoral values glorify anthropocentric agriculture and rigidly reject the possibility that nature has any independent integrity apart from man's imposed domestication.

Pastoral literature demonstrates the futility that must result from the full exploration of pastoral motives. The pastoral hero is never an image of human success or greatness, and he never achieves what he has been searching for. As his career begins in fear, self-pity, or self-indulgence, so in the end we are likely to see him "either dead or totally alienated from society, alone and powerless, like the evicted shepherd of Virgil's eclogue." [13] The pastoral epiphany is a recognition that neither society nor wilderness is a suitable environment for man, and that the garden which tries to mediate between the two merely separates him from both his fellow man and from nature.

Inherent contradictions in pastoral values lead typically to frustration and despair. The sensitive aristocrat who turns toward Arcadia and away from Rome often discovers that Rome is really within him. Though he can leave behind the fearsome environment of civilization and its cities, yet the psyche of civilization remains to guide his responses to nature. He cannot reject civilization without rejecting his own humanness, so he seeks a compromise in the halfway house of a pastoral Arcadia, somewhere midway between the horrors of wilderness and the horrors of the city. His choice of the garden-farm is this exact midpoint, a place of mediation between nature and civilization but also the point where the two worlds make contact and where both continually tug at him. His fear of wilderness is as intense as his fear of cities, and the garden merely intensifies the contrast without providing a solution. In his total alienation from both worlds, his only response is self-pity and despair at ever resolving the contradictions which he has now discovered to be internal as well as environmental. He cannot even achieve tragedy, for he has not risked enough. The end of the pastoral cycle is pathos.

PICARESQUE STRATEGIES

The picaresque world is a natural system in which man is one of the animal species. The picaro suffers from no conflict between society and nature simply because he sees society as one of the many forms of natural order. He objects to the society into which he is born no more than wolves or ants or whales object to theirs, and like these animals, he tries merely to adapt himself to his circumstances in the interests of survival—his own survival. He does not altruistically strive for the welfare of mankind, but merely lives his life as well as he can with little regard for distant idealisms. He is so completely absorbed as a participant in life that it never occurs to him to be a critic of it, or to escape into fantasies.

Picaresque nature is not a garden, but a wilderness. Its most obvious features are multiplicity and diversity, for within the picaresque world everything is tied to everything else according to complex interdependencies which defy simplification. Pain and pleasure are equally real, as are birth and death, peace and war, hunger and a full belly, love and hate. To attend to only one side of these polarities while rejecting the other would be to distort the truth, which the picaro knows he must not do if he hopes to endure. Instead, he takes each as it comes (often they come mixed) and deals with it according to its demands, enjoying the pleasant and enduring the painful as best he can. His world is an ecosystem and he is but one small organism within it. How he fits into the whole or what its purpose may be are beyond him, but he doesn't worry much about such questions.

The picaro's birth is generally obscure, often illegitimate, suggesting both his lack of social status and the absence of any sense of tradition or continuity with the past. The chaotic social environment in which he grows up has no niche prepared for him, and he soon discovers that he must create whatever success he can from the rawest of materials at hand. Early in life he goes on his own. His experiences quickly awaken him to the realization that no one will help him, that there is no obvious plan or order in the world, and that his survival or failure will depend upon his own inventiveness.

Lazarillo de Tormes, the Spanish novel already mentioned, is the prototype for later picaresque novels. Its hero, Lazarillo, is tricked and beaten by his first master and promptly achieves the realization that defines the picaresque perspective: "It is full time for me to open mine eyes, yea, and to provide and seek mine own advantage, considering that I am alone without any help." [14] Eyes wide open upon the world around him, looking to avoid danger and to exploit advantages, the picaro's life becomes a contest with the world, the only prizes for which are survival and an occasional hearty laugh. Lazarillo and the picaresque antiheroes modeled upon him live in spite of their surrounding social order, not because of it.

The picaresque hero perceives that the world is particularly dangerous to those who are weak, poor, or defenseless. The high moral and cultural values mouthed by powerful people are merely platitudes which do not in fact govern their actions and so they cannot be taken seriously. Those who live within the established social order are well fed, pious, educated in abstractions but often stupid in practical matters, and vindictive to all who do not conform to their ideals. The picaro is an outsider to this system, practical, clever, immoral, self-sufficient, and dedicated to making do by any means available. Staying alive is his most important goal, and having a good time comes second. He does not rebel against his society, nor does he try to reform it or to escape from it. Rather, he looks for weaknesses and loopholes in the system which he can use to his own advantage.

The picaro notes the chaotic complexity of society as keenly as his pastoral counterpart, but he reasons that he must meet it by becoming more complex himself, not by seeking simplicity. He learns early in his career that the elaborate mechanisms of social order do not serve his basic human needs, but that does not lead him to hate society. It simply means that he will have to assume full responsibility for his own welfare and that he can expect no help from others. The picaro is a man alone, not in the lofty and self-indulgent way of the pastoral hero, but in the modest manner of one who frankly assumes that no one cares about him. The problems around him seem too great to be solved or even understood, but since they were not of his making he need not feel guilty. He does need to live in the world that is defined by these problems, however, so he needs intelligence and wit.

The Reivers, by the twentieth-century American novelist, William Faulkner, is a pseudopicaresque novel. A statement made by the narrator of that novel could serve as a definition of picaresque intelligence:

I rate mules second only to rats in intelligence, the mule followed in order by cats, dogs, and horses last—assuming of course that you accept my definition of intelligence: which is the ability to cope with environment: which means to accept environment yet still retain at least something of personal liberty.[15]

The intelligence of mules, rats, and picaresque heroes is not directed toward puzzling out the rational elegance of pastoral utopias, but toward coping with the given circumstances of daily life. There is little room for nostalgia, fantasy, or for abstract intellectual speculation in the mind of the picaro, for he is occupied with present actions and events, and with the maintenance of his own precarious liberty.

The picaro is thus an opportunist rather than an escapist, a man of wit rather than of contemplation, a realist rather than an idealist. His commitment to endure must often be served by breaking or ignoring the laws and rules which his society has erected for communal protection. He is an outlaw and vulgar in the eyes of society's aristocrats.

Defensive Strategies

The world in which the picaro must make his way is often at war. Two picaresque war novels from different historical periods will illustrate the consistency of the picaresque genre: *Simplicius Simplicissimus* by the seventeenth-century German writer Johann Jacob Christoffel von Grimmelshausen, and *Catch-22* by the contemporary American novelist Joseph Heller. Grimmelshausen's *Simplicissimus* and Heller's *Catch-22* represent typical picaresque responses to the questions which war always raises: how can one live in a time of total social disruption, and what is one to do about the omnipresent threat of injury and death? The picaresque answers are always the same: adapt to circumstances and take evasive action.

What the black plague was to Boccaccio, the Thirty Years War (1618–1648) was to Grimmelshausen. All Europe suffered near total collapse of the civilized amenities, ostensibly over the resolution of religious differences between Protestants and Catholics. Grimmelshausen's picaresque novel begins with scenes of carnage and brutality which define the world in which the young Simplicius must make his way. "This introductory entertainment almost spoiled my desire to see the world," remarks Simplicius after witnessing the brutal destruction of his village by a cavalry troop: "If this is the way things are, the wilderness is far more attractive." [16] Though he tries to hide in the forest, events always force him back into the company of men, where he begins to learn the tricks of survival.

Like most picaresque novels, *Simplicissimus* represents a young man's initiation and education. Simplicius' first teacher is a minister whose message is that "the foolish world wants to be fooled. Use what intelligence they have left you . . . for your own advantage." [17] Intelligence in the service of deception is the picaro's basic strategy for survival. But the picaro deceives only so that he may save himself, never intentionally to injure others. Simplicius adopts whatever disguises seem appropriate in order to avoid trouble. His protective coloring makes him into a court jester, a minister, a soldier, a doctor, or an animal as his situation warrants. Each role saves him from some danger, and each teaches him something new by providing a fresh perspective upon events. Though he deceives others, he never gives in to the temptation to take his own disguises seriously.

The picaro does not treat his fantasies as if they were

realities, as pastoral heroes tend to do, but regards each new role as one possibility out of the many available to him, useful for solving a particular problem and perhaps interesting for the new insight it may offer, but in no way a limitation to be accepted. Picaresque life is not lived in search of the One True Way, but is rather an endless series of roles to be played in response to ever-changing circumstances.

Simplicius often compares himself to animals and even adopts animal disguises. He becomes a goose to avoid punishment, and later enjoys for some time the role of calf. As a talking animal he lectures his masters on the virtues of animals, praising them for their moderation, responsiveness to environment, and peacefulness compared to men.[18] Animals are congenial images to the picaro, for like him they live in the present and are not subject to self-deceptive illusions. Superior human mentality merely permits the picaro to become a better animal, not to transcend his animality.

The metaphysics of the picaresque world are relativistic and fluid. Simplicius early perceives that "nothing in the world is more constant than inconstancy."[19] Uncertainty and continuous change are not, however, oppressive to the picaro for he does not expect or admire permanence. Change means that the world consists of endlessly varied opportunities for new roles to be played and new advantages to be gained. Change may of course work to the picaro's disadvantage, as when Simplicius is transformed by smallpox from a handsome courtier admired by all the ladies to a pock-marked pariah, "so ugly that dogs would pee on me."[20] Neither condition is assumed to be definitive of his destiny or identity, but each is merely one more condition which must be explored for its potential. Simplicius merely adapts to his ugliness and learns to make his way by begging and fraud rather than by the seduction of wealthy ladies. Picaresque behavior is governed by an internalized acceptance of universal flux as the basic nature of the world. The picaro's philosophy is thus "to go with the times and make use of the inevitable." [21]

War is so often the setting for picaresque novels because its conditions intensify the problems to which the picaro must always adapt himself: rapid change, social disorder, irrationality, and the constant threat of injury or death. War merely exaggerates normal social conditions. It matters little whether it is the Thirty Years War or World War II, for in either case the personal problems of the picaro are the same. Joseph Heller's modern picaro, Yossarian, faces the same challenge as his counterpart Simplicius three centuries earlier: "It was all a sensible young gentleman like himself could do to maintain his perspective amid so much madness. And it was urgent that he did, for he knew his life was in danger." [22]

Yossarian struggles for survival in a world of aerial bombing rather than cavalry charges, but this merely means that his strategy must be more complex and quicker than that of Simplicius. Its principles are the same. Yossarian rejects the heroism expected of him in his role as an air force bombardier, preferring to survive as a coward: "He had decided to live forever or die in the attempt, and his only mission each time he went up was to come down alive." [23] He becomes a consummate master of the art of "evasive action," the erratic maneuvering of an airplane to avoid antiaircraft fire. Evasive action becomes a way of life for Yossarian whether on a bombing mission or on the ground, for his enemies are everywhere: "The enemy . . . is anybody who's going to get you killed, no matter *which* side he's on." [24] The American generals who plan bombing missions are as great a threat to his welfare as the German gunners who try to shoot him down. Questions of right and wrong, good and evil, friends and enemies dissolve into irrelevancy before the demanding task of survival in a world at war.

Evasive action means that Yossarian chooses to avoid danger rather than to destroy its source. In the picaresque manner, he assumes the state of his world to be a given condition that is beyond his power to improve. He accepts the irrational rules of war even when they change with every mission, and he tries to survive within them if possible. He lives from minute to minute, limiting his vision of the world to the cockpit or whorehouse or briefing room, each with its own threat to his welfare and challenge to his ingenuity which must somehow be met. Whatever the threat, he must adapt himself to its conditions with no hope of achieving peace and no idealistic delusions about his own capacity to triumph over adversity.

Ironically, Yossarian's evasions and fears are taken to be signs of his *failure* to adapt to the traditions of his culture. "You've been unable to adjust to the idea of war," his psychiatrist tells him. Yossarian agrees, then listens to a further exposition of the kind of adaptation that his society expects of him:

> "You have a morbid aversion to dying. You probably resent the fact that you're at war and might get your head blown off any second."
> "I more than resent it, sir. I'm absolutely incensed."
> "You have deep-seated survival anxieties. And you don't like bigots, bullies, snobs or hypocrites. Subconsciously there are many people you hate."

"Consciously, sir, consciously," Yossarian corrected in an effort to help. "I hate them consciously."

"You're antagonistic to the idea of being robbed, exploited, degraded, humiliated, or deceived. Misery depresses you. Ignorance depresses you. Persecution depresses you. Violence depresses you. Slums depress you. Greed depresses you. Crime depresses you. Corruption depresses you. You know, it wouldn't surprise me if you're a manic-depressive!"

"Yes, sir. Perhaps I am."

"Don't try to deny it."

"I'm not denying it, sir," said Yossarian, pleased with the miraculous rapport that finally existed between them. "I agree with all you've said."

"Then you admit you're crazy, do you?"

"Crazy?" Yossarian was shocked. "What are you talking about? Why am I crazy? You're the one who's crazy!" [25]

Picaresque sanity is recognition of the world's madness, not approval or emulation of it. The picaro cannot join forces with the agents of disaster and misery for he does not share their ideologies, but neither does he seek to destroy them. Rather than hating the source of evil, he has compassion for its victims, among whom he numbers himself. He is thus out of step with the dominant power structure, in relation to which his own actions seem insane. The picaro is a "rogue" because he refuses to endorse the ideologies of his time or their destructive consequences.

Yossarian is a responsible man, but not to the abstract values to which his corrupt society pays allegiance. Dignity, honor, morality, and patriotism are to the picaro the empty words behind which men hide their egotism, greed, vice, and treachery. His values are personal and existential. Yossarian in the end runs away from the war and its pretenses of heroic nobility, choosing instead to save his own life and to help another victim of violence, the kid sister of a Roman whore. When he is condemned as an escapist for evading his patriotic duties, Yossarian insists: "I'm not running *away* from my responsibilities. I'm running *to* them. There's nothing negative about running away to save my life. You know who the escapists are, don't you?" [26] The escapists, of course, are the people who lie to themselves about the perfectibility of man, the righteousness of warfare, the importance of their own egos, and the sanctity of conventional morality.

The picaresque evasion of pain is radically different from the pastoral retreat in search of peace. Picaresque peace is merely a temporary avoidance of danger, never the permanent security sought in pastoral literature. As Yossarian prepares to desert from the army at the end of *Catch-22,* his friends caution him that "no one will ever be on your side, and you'll always live in danger of betrayal." "I live that way now," replies Yossarian.[27] His future will be as dangerous as his past, but more on his own terms and with a better likelihood of survival than can be found within the war. Yossarian's life henceforth will be a calculated risk. When last seen, he is still running to avoid death.

Such inconclusive conclusions are typical of picaresque novels. The world's problems are never solved, no enemies are defeated, no new truth is realized, no peace is attained. In the course of the picaro's career he has gained only greater competence at survival, acceptance of responsibility for his own life, and a clearer understanding of the many threats which surround him.

Picaresque Artistry

Evasive picaresque action is not only a defensive posture; it has creative potential as well. The wit necessary to save the picaro's life in time of war is applicable to the creation of beauty in times of relative peace. As a master manipulator and creator of illusions, the picaro has much in common with the artist, a conjunction which is explored by the twentieth-century German novelist, Thomas Mann, in his picaresque novel, *Confessions of Felix Krull, Confidence Man.*

As a young man, Felix Krull ponders the implications of various available perspectives upon the world. Great heroes and empire builders, he reasons, must see the world as a small place, like a chessboard upon which they expect to win their identity by managing the various pieces. The world of saints and hermits must also be a small and insignificant place from which it is best to withdraw in the hope of discovering a better one through mental fantasy or religious transcendence. Krull prefers to see the world as "a great and infinitely enticing phenomenon, offering priceless satisfactions and worthy in the highest degree of all my efforts and solicitude." [28] The vastness and complexity of the world is for Krull an endless source of opportunity for exploring his own potentials and talents. His motive is neither mastery of the world nor escape from its conditions, but the full utilization of his own talents to create a life rivaling the world itself in variety and excellence.

"He who really loves the world shapes himself to please it" [29] is Krull's motto, which defines his strategy as a member of society and as an artist. Adaptation to the given conditions of reality becomes more than the defensive technique of wartime picaros, for Krull regards himself as material to be shaped according to the potential richness and beauty of his circumstances. It is not the world which must be made to suit man's pleasures, but man to suit the world's. This does not mean merely meeting the expectations of other men, for Krull's conception of the world is not bounded by his contemporary society but includes as well the total context of natural and human history. The world he seeks to please includes both nature and man.

In order to please the world, it is often necessary to disappoint the expectations of contemporary society. Krull bends and breaks the conventions of his social context when they prevent him from exploiting his potential for creative experimentation. His idea of aristocracy, for instance, is based upon the observation that nature provides a graded hierarchy of beings according to innate gifts of talent and beauty. He early perceives that nature has endowed him with both: "I could not conceal from myself that I was made of superior stuff." [30] Yet his modest social position does not conform to his natural gifts, for society grades its members according to the artificial criteria of wealth and family, both of which are accidental. In order to bring his social position into agreement with his innate superiority, therefore, he acquires money and rank by means of theft and deception.

There is no bitterness or greed involved in these acts, and Krull is careful to see that no one is hurt by them. His technique is to make himself so pleasing and attractive to others that they are moved to grant him favors, so that while he profits they do not lose but give to him willingly. His fortune is acquired from a wealthy woman, slightly perverse, who gets a sexual thrill from being robbed of her jewels by a handsome young man, and his aristocratic rank is bestowed upon

him by a profligate marquis whose identity Krull takes over
in order to leave the young nobleman free to pursue anon-
ymously his love affair with an actress. In spite of his unfortunately obscure birth, Krull thus earns the social credentials of superiority which correspond to his innate excellence.

If social standards are false they must be corrected—not
for everyone, for that would produce equal falsity—but in
particular instances. Krull is consistent with the picaresque
code in his acceptance of the given social order, and in his
belief that rank and order are natural hierarchical systems,
not false social conventions. He rejects, for instance, the notion that nudity is democratic in that it abolishes the social
ranks established by clothing styles. On the contrary, he
argues, "Nakedness can only be called just in so far as it
proclaims the naturally unjust constitution of the human
race, unjust in that it is aristocratic." [31] Clothing displays
false social status; its absence abolishes only the falsity and
proclaims the natural rank order based upon beauty and
agility of body.

The picaro is never a rebel against society, but merely
a manipulator of its conditions for his own welfare in accordance with the principles of nature. When asked if he is a
socialist, Krull answers, "No, indeed! . . . I find society
enchanting just as it is and am on fire to earn its good
opinion." [32] Of course he earns society's admiration by
deception and illusion, thus earning also the title rogue,
but his deceptions resemble those of art more than those of
crime. He is an actor portraying the roles appropriate to his
context at a given moment: "I seemed not only able to put
on whatever social rank or personal characteristics I chose,
but could actually adapt myself to any given period or

century." [33] His social roles as elevator boy, waiter, pimp, nobleman are played in order to fulfill the potential inherent in each role, not only to serve Krull's personal needs. He is a professional illusionist glorying in his adaptive skill.

Yet for all his admiration of society, his life remains by choice alone and isolated. Isolation is a necessary condition of picaresque action which emphasizes the dependence of the picaro upon his own devices. And it is not a cause for sorrow, as it is for the pastoral hero, but rather an opportunity. The picaro takes pride in his independence, even though it requires some sacrifice of personal intimacy. Krull accepts the fact that "close associations, friendship, and companionship were not to be my lot, but that I should instead be inescapably compelled to follow my strange path alone, dependent entirely upon myself, rigorously self-sufficient." [34] Though he remains on a congenial footing with those around him and even proves to be a master lover with women, Krull never permits intimacy to progress to the point of a dependency which might restrict his freedom to respond to new threats or opportunities.

Picaresque life is animal existence augmented by the imaginative and adaptive powers of the human mind. Unlike the pastoral mode, in which the mind is used to create alternatives to a dangerous present reality, the picaresque mode expresses acceptance of the present and adaptation to its conditions without concern for abstract ideologies or sentimental moralities. The comparison of the hero to animals, an almost universal feature of picaresque fiction, emphasizes the picaro's acceptance of biological limitations which define the nature of life and suggest the proper purposes which should govern man's use of his intellect. Faulkner's rats and mules, Grimmelshausen's calf and goose, and the many other animals which recur in picaresque literary art are most often used as models of appropriate action rather than as images of debased life which threaten some conventional standard of human dignity.

The final chapters of Mann's *Felix Krull* are devoted to the hero's exploration of his own relationship to animal and biological existence as he is conducted through the Lisbon Museum of Natural History by its director. The first animal Krull sees inside the museum is a magnificent white stag mounted against a forest background. He enjoys the likeness between himself and the stag, not only because both are well-formed and beautiful, but also because of their common attitude toward their environments. Stag and Krull are "dignified and alert . . . calm yet wary," and ready to "disappear at a bound into the darkness" at the slightest sign of danger.[35] The stag is a handsome picaro, adept at evasive action like his human counterpart Felix Krull.

The record of evolution displayed in the museum further shows Krull his kinship with the animals as well as his separation from them. He sees "the contrast between my own fineness and elegance and the primitive crudity of many of the uncanny-looking fossils, the primitive crustaceans, cephalopods, brachiopods, tremendously ancient sponges and entrail-less lily-stars. . . . These first beginnings, however absurd and lacking in dignity and usefulness, were preliminary moves in the direction of me—that is, of Man."[36] Higher evolutionary forms, mammals and primates, further confirm Krull's joy at his new-found unity with all animal life, "in the end they all prefigured me, even though disguised as in some sorry jest."[37] When his tour brings him to the displays of early humans, his pleasure in evolutionary continuity is further confirmed, for in primitive man he sees "what had been striving toward me from the grey reaches of antiquity." [38] He is confirmed in the perception that he had earlier derived from his conversations with the museum director: "Men are descended from animals in just about the same way that the organic is descended from the inorganic. Something was added." [39] Consciousness was added, the gift which augments the process of evolution but does not separate man from that process.

Consciousness permits man to enjoy his animal powers and beauties more than the other animals can. As Krull sees it, man does by will only what lower animals do by instinct, and so man becomes responsible for what he is. Crude animals cannot be blamed for their ugliness, but among men it is "culpable to be ugly." Krull finds it "a kind of carelessness" which offends him and which contrasts sharply with his own artistic attitude toward himself: "Out of innate consideration for the world that was awaiting me, I took care while I was being formed that I should not offend its eyes. . . . I'd call it a kind of self-discipline." [40] Krull has here restated the law of creative picaresque behavior with which his career began: "He who really loves the world shapes himself to please it."

Consciousness, intelligence, language, imagination—these specifically human attributes are to the picaro the means for artistic adaptation of himself to his environment. He uses his gifts for self-defense and for more intense enjoyment of his surroundings. Dominance over his environment is not his goal, nor is he tempted to use his imaginative powers for the creation of idealistic fantasies. Accepting the accidents of natural and social history which have produced him and the environment which defines his possibilities, the picaro applies his intelligence to making the most of whatever nature or society may have to offer.

Picaresque Politics

Picaresque strategy, like pastoral fantasy, is applicable to politics as well as to personal life. If Thomas Jefferson is the political theorist of pastoral values, the Florentine statesman and diplomat Niccolò Machiavelli (1469–1527) is the spokesman for picaresque politics. Jefferson tried to establish a political order which, like a garden, would nourish what is good and beautiful and banish the evil and ugly. Machiavelli's politics permits the accommodation of both pleasant and unpleasant realities. In *The Prince* (published 1532), Machiavelli accepts the fact that the civilized world is often a nasty place, particularly for those who try to be virtuous: "A man who wishes to make a profession of goodness in everything must necessarily come to grief among so many who are not good." [41] Such a realization is often the impetus for the pastoral hero to retreat to a safer place, but for Machiavelli it is the basis for a strategy of survival: "Therefore it is necessary . . . to learn how not to be good, and to use this knowledge and not use it, according to the necessity of the case." [42] Machiavelli is not advocating evil, of course, but merely allowing for it in his scheme of things and implicitly arguing that political survival is more important to the state than ethical propriety. He later suggests that a successful prince must "not deviate from what is good, if possible, but be able to do evil if constrained." [43]

Like a picaresque hero, Machiavelli's prince is advised to model his behavior upon animal techniques of survival.

After reminding us that ancient heroes were often educated by centaurs in order to unite in them the best features of men and animals, Machiavelli suggests that a clever leader "must imitate the fox and the lion, for the lion cannot protect himself from traps, and the fox cannot defend himself from wolves. One must therefore be a fox to recognize traps, and a lion to frighten wolves." [44] Animals can show men how to be agile, evasive, and terrifying to enemies, but Machievelli does not look to them for lessons in how to kill. The lion's power is useful for frightening the enemy, but strictly human means are used when it is necessary to kill him. Killing is not Machiavelli's purpose, but self-preservation is. When the prince maintains himself he also protects the integrity of society.

No utopia is possible for Machiavelli, for he does not regard the problems of life as solvable. "This is found in the nature of things, that one never tries to avoid one difficulty without running into another, but prudence consists in being able to know the nature of the difficulties, and taking the least harmful as good." [45] Pragmatic endurance in the face of adversity is the best that can be hoped for, and it can be achieved only by accepting the accidental circumstances of life as given conditions which must be dealt with. Human welfare consists in clear-eyed attentiveness to the needs of a changing environment and adaptation of behavior to fit those needs, for men are successful "so long as their ways conform to circumstances, but when they are opposed then they are unsuccessful." [46]

No eternal power will defend man or assure his success, but only his own accuracy in reading the temper of time and events and modifying himself in accordance with necessity. Machiavelli's prince is as alone in the world as any picaresque hero, with only himself to look to for protection against danger, for "only those defenses are good, certain and durable, which depend upon yourself alone and your own ability." [47]

Unimaginative and power-hungry political leaders have long misused Machiavelli's comic-picaresque techniques in the service of their own tragic-pastoral values. Ambitious people in public office use deception and subterfuge more often for the aggrandizement of their personal egos than for the survival and welfare of their states and their people. The Watergate scandal and its many historical precedents are examples of how easy it is to misapply Machiavelli's ideas to Jefferson's goals. Machiavelli's picaresque politics are not designed to glorify personalities, to conquer nature, or to serve honor and abstract morality, all of which are tragic values and pastoral passions. Instead, the picaro Machiavelli offers instruction in the comic spirit which begins from the need to survive and reaches toward an artistic adaptation of political affairs to the natural conditions of life.

Neither Machiavelli nor the picaros of literature have ever been respectable examples of moral propriety. They explicitly reject the idealistic conventions of their culture because they have found them to be hazardous to life. They do not pretend to offer models of proper moral behavior, but only strategies for survival. Picaresque art and politics are mildly discomforting perhaps because they mirror the principles by which so many people actually live, however much they may feel that they should not. They demonstrate the discrepancy between abstract precepts and concrete actions. The insight they offer into the human condition is thus neither flattering nor comforting, though they can be enjoyed for their assertion that imaginative intelligence and durability are the most important characteristics of our species.

ROGUES VERSUS SAINTS

The roots of pastoral and picaresque go deeply into Western cultural traditions, the collective psyche, and perhaps into human evolutionary origins. It is not easy to tell whether the two modes reflect differences in human temperament and personality or are expressions of contradictory ideologies which may earn our conscious assent or rejection. The pastoral mode seems to be tantamount to an ideology, for writers in this mode generally claim to know how men should live and expect them to mend their ways in order to attain desirable goals; they assume life to be perfectible, however great their despair at the discovery that men often reject their chances for perfection. The picaresque, on the other hand, is descriptive rather than prescriptive. Picaresque works are not much help in the search for what ought to be because they are concerned only with what is. They offer a mirror of human behavior, not a model for imitation.

Pastoral man is born an aristocrat, superior in his social status over other men and thoroughly civilized. He considers himself superior to other men and sees mankind as a whole superior to nature. His anthropocentric world exists for the purpose of perfecting human welfare and elevating the human spirit. Confident that he is at the center of creation, he yet sees the failure of his fellow men to achieve their potential and he is oppressed by it. He regretfully turns away from his society and its unnecessary miseries, accepts his isolation as a painful consequence, and looks for renewal from nature itself. Society may stupidly damage the god-given nobility of mankind, but nature is expected to re-affirm it through her pastoral hero.

Picaresque man begins life with no credentials of dignity. Neither his social position nor his metaphysics support a claim to an a priori superiority over anything. His main concern is not status but survival. He quickly learns that survival is a competitive process requiring that the immediate environment be taken seriously for both its threats and its opportunities. Since he is ignorant of any plans the world may have for him, he is free to become whatever seems appropriate or interesting. He knows nothing about man's potential and he has not heard that man must transcend nature in order to achieve his destined dignity, so he lives like an animal in the world where he has accidently appeared, interested only in what the present may hold for him.

Morality is a cornerstone of pastoral life. Man is assumed to be naturally good, and if he nevertheless seems corrupt it must be because the institutions of civilization have made him so. The experience of nature is therapeutic, restoring him to the state of natural goodness with which he began. In pastoral literature the nobility of savages is extolled and mankind is urged to regain the purity that has been sacri-ficed to civilization.

The picaresque vision reveals the savagery of nobility, disclosing early that exalted moral postures or social am-bitions usually lead quickly to someone's death or undoing. Morality is dangerous to the picaro; if he adopts it in his own life he will be committing himself in advance to courses of action which may be inappropriate in some unforseeable future, and if he obeys the moral injunctions of others he may simply have to suffer the consequences in their stead. Picaresque man is a mixed bag of good and evil unable to sort himself out or to decide which is his most significant attribute. He is skeptical of all moral abstractions or systematic rules, and he has no idea what man is by nature or in the eyes of God. If survival is a moral principle, he is inclined in its favor.

Pastoral emotions tend toward the melodramatic. Self-pity is a common beginning for pastoral narrative. The hero is despondent because the world has not treated him as he deserves. He finds solace in nostalgic fantasies about the good old days of his own youth or of mankind's in the Garden of Eden. His belief that life has been beautiful inspires him with hope that it can be good again if only he can restore the proper conditions. The pastoral quest is a sentimental journey away from present pain in search of past peace. It is seldom a successful quest. The emotional cycle of pastoral experience normally moves from nostalgia to hope, to disillusionment, to final despair.

Compassion for suffering is probably the most serious emotion experienced by picaresque heroes. The picaro makes little distinction between his own misfortune and that of others around him, treating both with solicitude and resignation. He sees pain as the consequence of his own errors rather than as evidence of the world's malice, so he is likely to be self-mocking rather than self-pitying. He more often laughs at the world's absurdities than cries over its inequities. As he has no hope, he need never suffer despair. His career does not proceed in a cycle, but is merely an account of his increasingly adept durability as he responds to ever-new circumstances. Picaresque narratives do not reach conclusions and their heroes never achieve either fulfillment or discovery, for the picaresque mode presents life as a continuous process, endlessly repetitious and perhaps meaningless, but interesting.

Pastoral life is polarized, presenting mutually exclusive alternatives between which a choice must be made. The good must be achieved, the evil rooted out; peace is excellent, war is hell; elegant simplicity is preferable to unpleasant complexity; purity is man's goal, pollution his punishment; society is corrupt but nature is sinless. Pastoral motivation is always in the direction of positive goals which are believed to be attainable if only their opposites can be avoided. The pastoral world is a battleground between God and Satan, and the pastoral hero is enlisted among the angels. He is, to be sure, a rear-echelon angel not involved in the battle itself, but he prays fervently for God's side to win.

The picaro does not positively search for peace but merely hopes to avoid war. He is rarely able to distinguish between good and evil except in their simplest forms, pleasure and pain—and even these are often mixed. His world is plural rather than polar. Many gods, many satans, and many of indeterminate moral status contend before his eyes, each holding both threats and promises and displaying several neutral shades in between. If he were given the opportunity to make the world over again he would not know where to begin. It is not the world that must meet his conditions, but he its. His constant motivation is to blend himself into events and circumstances of whatever kind.

Images of environment and metaphors of behavior reflect the separate value systems of pastoral and picaresque modes. Garden and farm supply the dominant figures in the pastoral mode, wilderness and the city in the picaresque. These images have carried far beyond their literary origins and

114

represent influential concepts of intellectual life, particularly in contemporary attitudes toward the natural environment.

Botany dominates the pastoral scene. Plants symbolize the kind of life most desired by the pastoral seeker: rooted, placid, and beautiful. The only animals admitted to pastoral landscapes are those domestic creatures whose behavior is similarly calm; nervous and aggressive animals are carefully fenced out. The pastoral psyche yearns for the peace of vegetative existence. A scene from *Catch-22* illustrates both the desirability and the unpleasant consequences of botanical life. Near the end of the novel, Yossarian's friend Danby wishes that he were a plant:

> "It must be nice to live like a vegetable," he conceded wistfully.
>
> "It's lousy," answered Yossarian.
>
> "No, it must be very pleasant to be free from all this doubt and pressure," insisted Major Danby. "I think I'd like to live like a vegetable and make no important decisions."
>
> "What kind of vegetable, Danby?"
>
> "A cucumber or carrot."
>
> "What kind of cucumber? A good one or a bad one?"
>
> "Oh, a good one, of course."
>
> "They'd cut you off in your prime and slice you up for a salad."
>
> Major Danby's face fell. "A poor one, then."
>
> "They'd let you rot and use you for fertilizer to help the good ones grow."
>
> "I guess I don't want to live like a vegetable, then," said Major Danby with a smile of sad resignation.[48]

For all their peacefulness, vegetables and pastoral heroes are victims of the needs, desires, and callousness of non-vegetables. Danby's scene is a miniature parody of the typical stages of pastoral narrative: the desire to retreat to simpler life, the recognition of helplessness before the world's demands, and the final moment of sad resignation. The attempt to achieve the values of the garden—nourishment, beauty, peacefulness, and stability—leads inevitably to disappointment in a perverse and competitive world.

The picaresque wilderness, of course, also leads to no great goals, but since the picaro has no expectations he can hardly be disappointed about that. Picaresque literature does not express the kind of hopelessness implied by tragedy and existential despair, for these traditions seem to hold the world responsible for being reasonable and just to humans, and regard its failures as somehow a personal affront to mankind. The picaro is hopeless only in the sense that he sees hope to be an irrelevant concept, an unjustifiable expectation of the future which offers no help in dealing with present problems. The picaro's only "hope" is that he may succeed at the day-to-day business of keeping himself alive; if a wolf can be said to hope for a meal each day and the avoidance of trappers who want his pelt, then the picaro can be said to hope. In the picaresque tradition, man is shown living as animals live, confronting the present defensively and opportunistically, without expectations or illusions, proud of strength but accurately aware of its limitations, mistrustful but not malicious, and above all adaptive to the immediate environment.

Perhaps the major difference between pastoral and picaresque lies in the application each makes of human intelligence. The pastoral intellect uses the rational capacity of the mind to criticize the inadequacies of present experience and its imaginative talents to create alternatives to the present. It is characterized by abstract ideas—truth,

justice, goodness, love—intended to lead man toward a fulfillment of his potential at some future time, guided also by
the accumulated wisdom of the past. The picaresque intellect instead concentrates its analytical powers upon the
study of immediate reality, and its imagination upon the
creation of strategies for survival. Picaresque liberty is not
escape from misfortune, but confidence in one's ability to
persist in spite of it.

Two of the major concerns of civilization have been the
conquest of nature and the search for social order among
men. Both appear now to be nearing a final stage under the
names of environmental crisis and urban crisis. Human
management of both problems has been governed by values
familiar to the pastoral tradition. Cities have labored to
achieve ideals of human order with an almost universal
agreement that their present is hopelessly inadequate. As
dreams of human peace have again and again proved hollow,
we have taken some comfort in our ability to subdue the
dangers of nature and to farm the earth more efficiently.
Now even our success over nature threatens us, for we
are discovering that the most sophisticated of gardens is yet
inadequate to sustain life. Expelled from the garden and
unable to live in the city, we are near the despair which
commonly ends the pastoral cycle. The world has refused
to adapt itself to our wishes.

The disreputable picaro shows us only how to tailor our
needs to the resources available in the world. Accepting
both nature and society as given and unalterable conditions,
the picaresque mode of action concentrates upon the comic
task of encouraging life wherever it is found and avoiding
death from whatever quarter. If the picaresque lacks morality and idealism, it is capable of pride and beauty and vig-

117

orous practical intelligence, not to mention good-natured humor. It ignores the human desire to discover what man ought to be, and it defines what man is in very modest terms. In the interest of survival, the human race might be wise to settle for that.

SIX

Ecological
Esthetics

THEORIES OF HUMAN ART AND BEHAVIOR IMPERFECTLY RE-
flect actual practices. Intellectual explanations are always
less rich and diverse than the artistic or ethical activities
they attempt to explain. Such academic speculations are
expressions of the contemporary social and intellectual environments in which they are formulated. They represent
the perspectives of particular periods in human history, not
characteristics of the human species. The study of theory
is thus the study of changing circumstances in the thinking
human mind, but not of the world at large which extends
beyond humanity. Both art and ethical behavior are much
larger than the theories invented to make sense of them.
Beauty is always more than philosophers of esthetics can
account for, and ethical behavior is never comprehended by
the ideas and laws devised for it. This chapter and the next
will measure some of the gaps between human experience
and human ideas about esthetics and ethics.

The history of theoretical esthetics has been dominated
by the great "art versus nature" debate which begins with

Plato's assertion that all artistic creations are imperfect, often deceptive, approximations of reality. The most extreme version of this point of view is that art is somehow a dishonest corruption of nature, an inspired lie: the word *art* itself is the major etymological element in *artificiality*. Following this line of thought, esthetic theory has traditionally emphasized the separation of artistic from natural creation, assuming that art was the "higher" or "spiritualized" product of the human soul and not to be confused with the "lower" or "animal" world of biology. Tough-minded people often look upon art as "unnatural" while idealistic humanists see in art an image of man's spiritual transcendence over nature. Both views distort the relationship between nature and art.

Darwin's revelations concerning evolution compelled closer scrutiny of biological processes, and consequently the realization that traditional anthropocentric thinking has simultaneously overestimated human spirituality and underestimated biological complexity. Plants and animals are much more closely related to man than had been previously realized. Philosophers who have recognized this new closeness of biology and humanity have begun in the last century to attempt a reevaluation of esthetic theory in the light of new biological knowledge. The result has been the revision of such old concepts as "organic form" in order to suggest that artistic forms somehow achieve excellence as they more closely approximate the structural integrity of biological organisms. Works of art are likened to bodies, with an anatomy and physiology of their own, and a corresponding state of health or disease which depends upon their internal equilibrium. This has proved to be a productive line of thinking, and it has gone a long way toward overcoming the false dichotomy between nature and art which has dominated esthetic theory. Yet the comparison of a work of art to the structure of an individual body is still too simple, and it accounts for only some kinds of esthetic experience.

The preferred body for such a comparison, of course, is generally the human body. Esthetic theory has retained an almost exclusive interest in mankind, even while admitting the relevance of biological life to artistic creativeness. Humans seem willing to admit only those comparisons between biological form and artistic form which retain our preferred image of human centrality. When man gave up anthropomorphizing nature and began instead to zoomorphize art, he still managed to keep man in the spotlight.

The Underprivileged Animal

According to one ancient Greek account of creation, the careless god Epimetheus was given the responsibility for distributing the ingredients of biological creation among all the creatures, and he botched the job. Epimetheus lavished upon the wild animals gifts of beautiful fur and feathers, gracefulness of form, strength, and agility, to such an extent that he ran out of desirable characteristics by the time he came to man. His big brother Prometheus, mankind's special friend, then saved man from shame by endowing him with the tools of dominance over the other animals even though he was weaker and uglier than they. Like many since, Prometheus reasoned that a creature equipped with language and technology could get along well enough without beauty.

Other Greeks, as well as Hebrews and Christians, have preferred to think that the human body differs from wild animal forms because of its likeness to divinity. One of the assumptions of the Western humanistic tradition is that man is made in the image of God; adherents of that tradition found it difficult to swallow the notion that humans are underprivileged animals. Humanistic art from all periods seems to put the human form at the apex of all creation—presumably by virtue of its superior beauty. Such flattery has a convincing quality to it, and makes it easy to forget our tendency to borrow fur and feathers from wild animals when we want to adorn our bodies, and to ignore the repulsion that we often feel when looking upon our own kind. It is much easier to see a resemblance between man and God in the works of Michelangelo than in the faces and bodies of our neighbors.

Recent morphological studies of animals make it possible to review this old problem from new perspectives, and to reevaluate the relationship between organic forms in biology and in art. It has become evident, for instance, that domestication produces a fairly regular pattern of changes in the structure and appearance of wild animals. These include such skeletal changes as shortened extremities, spinal deformities that produce a stooped posture, and often bowed legs. Skull modifications typically include irregularities of the nose and chin, cranial distortion, and shortening of the skull base. Bodily connective tissues are also reduced in tension, causing drooping ears, flabby skin, and a general decrease of muscular agility. There is a marked tendency toward obesity in domesticated animals, producing the hanging stomach so characteristic of many farm animals. These features of domestication apparently remain remarkably constant over a wide range of different domesticated species.[1]

Konrad Lorenz has observed that "our emotional value

judgment categorizes as repulsive characters which have arisen through typical domestication effects . . . virtually all characters which we perceive as specifically ugly are genuine domestication effects." [2] Lorenz traces domestication characteristics to the decreased influence of evolutionary selection among domesticated animals, and points out that any species freed from the pressures of natural selection is likely to develop the physical characteristics of domestication, including such species as the European cave bear which ruled with unquestioned dominance during the late Pleistocene, and more recently, man.

The human body may share more features with the animals of the barnyard than with those of the forest, sea, or air. What we have imposed upon other animals for agricultural reasons, we have also imposed upon ourselves through civilization. Yet the products of human self-domestication do not generally please us esthetically. For all our pride in the human body and in the effects of civilization, when people try to represent beauty—in art or in fashion—they generally conceal their own characteristics of domestication and emphasize those shared with, or borrowed from, the free-living wild animals. Even the most dedicated humanistic artists of classical Greece or Renaissance Italy have found wild features beautiful and domesticated features ugly.

The motive behind the Epimetheus story is not simple misanthropy, but an attempt to explain the remarkable fact that wild animals are often more esthetically pleasing to humans than their own species. Despite the massive counter-influence of humanistic esthetics and artistic glorification of the human body, humans cannot honestly conceal a gnawing awareness that they are not the handsomest creatures in the world. Even if that fact were to be openly admitted, there would be the problem of explaining it, as human conceptions of beauty and ugliness must be based to some extent on self-contemplation. Clearly if the human body is a proper standard of beauty against which all esthetic judgments must be measured, only certain *artistic representations* of the body meet the criteria; few people find esthetic pleasure in the body they see in a full-length mirror. Artistic creations intended to represent human beauty normally suppress domestication characteristics and exaggerate those features which are common to free-living animals: long legs, tight muscles, angular and expressive facial features, well-shaped heads, small stomachs. Domestication features are reproduced only when the intention is to ridicule mankind as Bosch and Goya did in painting, and as Jonathan Swift did when his Gulliver met the Yahoos, a repulsive species of domesticated humans kept by wild horses. The preferred subject for art has always been the human body in its wild state, free of the effects of domestication which most of us carry to work each day wrapped in clothing designed to conceal as many of our typical domestication defects as possible. Domesticated man is a fit subject only for grotesque art.

The Biology of Beauty

Some of the perennial unsolved questions of esthetics are: How is it possible to account at all for a distinction between ugliness and beauty? Why should there be such categories, and from what sources might they arise? Theorists of art who do not look to man as a focus of beauty have often looked to something called "nature," though there is much disagreement about the meaning of the term. Esthetic theory may be more successful in defining beauty when it has incorporated some of the conceptions of nature and its processes which have been formulated by contemporary biologists and ecologists.

The problems posed by temporal beauty and spatial beauty may be considered separately, for biology and esthetics seem to agree that slightly different principles apply in each category, allowing for considerable overlap. The spatial or visual arts—painting, sculpture, design—are best compared to organic physical structures in nature, while the temporal arts—notably literature and music—are best illuminated from the perspective of biological processes as they are understood to act in the temporal schemes of evolution and ecological succession.

As an abstract concept, form is both temporal and spatial, consisting of both process and structure. Structure displays the process of composition by which a given form has come into being. An interest in intricate seashell designs, patterns of windblown sand, or the pleasing network of lines on a leaf will probably lead to curiosity about how such forms were created. Scientific analysis then seeks to unfold the pattern of events which produced the form. The same approach may be taken toward a work of visual art. In examining a painting or a piece of sculpture, it is often helpful to inquire into its historical and social context and into the artist's biography and methods of composition. Whatever method of analysis is used, it is the compelling experience of an apparently complete form which motivates the interest.

Human bodily equipment includes no organ that is responsive to time in the way that sight and touch respond to space. The "sense of time" is not a sense at all but rather an idea derived from the awareness of change and movement in space. One cannot "see" process in the things of nature or in visual art; instead one sees structure, a finished form, and it is only upon reflection that the structure is realized to be the result of a process. As Paul Weiss, emeritus neurobiologist at Rockefeller University has put it: "Organic form is frozen development; formal beauty reflects developmental order." [3]

Professor Weiss has analyzed in detail the visual forms in nature which evoke esthetic responses. His provocative study argues that the human perception of beauty is in fact a recognition of systems of order in things, whether the things in question are the products of biological growth or of human artistic creation. After surveying scores of structural patterns from biological and artistic history, Professor Weiss concludes that "the common pattern of appeal we have discovered in these manifold patterns is their non-randomness—the presence of some rule of ordered distribution of units." [4] He is careful to specify, however, that nonrandomness is not to be confused with static or mechanically precise concepts of absolute regularity; the order of living forms is "order with tolerances":

> True organic order, as we know it, sets only the general frame and pattern, leaving the precise ways of execution adjustable, and, to this extent, indeterminate. Esthetically, the principle finds expression in the superiority of handicraft, with no two objects wholly congruous, over the monotony of serial machine production. Biologically, it manifests itself in the superiority of laws of development which prescribe only the mode of procedure but leave the actual execution free to adapt itself to the exigencies of a world whose details are themselves unpredictable. [5]

Beauty, Weiss finds, is a perception of the order appropriate to the complicated experiences of life; perfect mathematical regularity is an abstract creation of the human mind which suggests the absence of life.

An analysis strikingly similar to Weiss's is to be found in Susanne Langer's landmark study of esthetics, *Feeling and Form,* which appeared at about the same time as Professor Weiss's "Beauty and the Beast." [6] Miss Langer is an esthetician and a philosopher, distinctly a humanist by professional training if not by creed. Her discussion of visual art draws as heavily upon biological forms in nature as does that of Weiss, and for the same reasons: both agree that human esthetic responses are intelligible only if it is possible to find the common element that governs human perceptions of beauty in natural forms and in human art forms. They agree also that the name of that common element is life, genuine biological life with its intricate structures and broad freedoms. Biology is the study of life itself, and esthetics is the study of the illusions of life created symbolically by man. "Living form" in art, concludes Professor Langer, is alive in a biological sense; that is, it is capable of broad growth and adaptability, but in her view it also adds an important new force: "It *expresses* life—feeling, growth, movement, emotion, and everything that characterizes vital existence." [7] It is only at this point that Professors Weiss and Langer seem to part company, for here they differ not in their perception of the elements in common between art and nature, but in their identification of the characteristics within humans which respond to both.

Perhaps it is no surprise to find that a scientist associates beauty with the orderliness of nature, or that a philosopher finds beauty to lie in nature's capacity for expressing human emotions. It is customary to distinguish between intellectual and emotional life, generally including science in the former and art in the latter. Weiss's emphasis upon biological order and Langer's upon human emotion are not, of course, mutually exclusive, but merely variant ways to describe the human values attached to perceived forms. The two positions differ in the *locus* of esthetic experience assumed by each: for Weiss, beauty is a property inherent in things; for Langer, beauty exists in the human response to things. Their difference in emphasis is symptomatic and important, and will be returned to later. For now it is enough to note that both demonstrate exhaustively, using independent methods and examples, that human esthetic pleasure in visual forms depends upon the biological integrity of the forms perceived. Images of organic life are visually beautiful in nature or in art.

Time as Bioesthetic Structure

Temporal art resembles an ecosystem more closely than it resembles an organism. Works of literature and music are chronologically unified, integrating varied forces according to the processes governing their development. Literature and music offer an experience of *time itself* in its manifold process of change and growth. We do not see the structure of a poem, a novel, or a sonata, but rather experience its form sequentially as it unfolds before us. The appeal of temporal art is thus partly attributable to human curiosity about how things are going to turn out, and the final satisfaction is a recognition that a process has been fulfilled in time. Great temporal art includes multiple processes of varying kinds which proceed simultaneously toward a resolution, as in the intricacies of a Bach fugue or an epic poem with its multileveled themes and characters.

An ecosystem similarly achieves biological stability by integrating a great number of organisms and processes in a state of maximum adaptation to a given environment which is constantly changing. It achieves beauty in precisely the same way—or rather, the human perception of its beauty is indistinguishable from our recognition of its biological integrity. A beautiful landscape is one in which the processes of life, including of course death and pain as well as birth and growth, are provided for in all their complexity. Perhaps there is a common ground between the delight found in temporal art and the delight found in the stable processes of a biological ecosystem. When we admire a wilderness landscape we are responding to a complex image of processes which are readily associated with human well-being. A burned forest is ugly because it represents a truncated system of growth, but a rich mixture of trees, grass, and wildlife is a working system that is productively oriented in time.

The perception of temporal complexity is one of the unique talents of the enlarged human brain. The great achievement of language is that it gives people a means to comprehend past and future events, and allows them to record—or to invent—processes of change which occur over long periods of time. These capacities were highly developed in man long before he began to recognize intricacy in the processes of nature. Only since the study of evolution and ecological succession in the past century has science developed the analytical tools permitting the study of high orders of temporal intricacy in a relatively systematic manner. Historically, the human appreciation of temporal form has been intuitive, and its most effective media have been literature and music.

Many theoretical conceptions suited to the analysis of temporal complexity derive from ancient attempts to understand temporal art. Temporal form is a familiar concept in musical and literary criticism where it has always been necessary to identify the unities produced from the interactions of widely diverse processes within a given time scale. Ecological investigation is a new attempt to deal systematically with time as works of art have always dealt with it: as formed process.

Balance in Ecology and Art

Works of art are gratifying because they offer an integrative experience, bringing highly diversified elements together into a balanced whole. A great work of art resembles an ecosystem in that it conveys a unitive experience. It is not important that each element be pleasing in itself, but it is essential that the relationship established among elements be true and consistent within the system as a whole. Literature includes much pain and degradation, and music incorporates dissonance within the beauty of the whole. It is necessary that works of art include a full range of pleasant and unpleasant experiences in order to be esthetically satisfying. The ultimate success of a work of art depends on the finished artistic system as a whole and the fidelity of that system to a complex integrity which includes all creative and destructive forces in balanced equilibrium.

As human perceptions of ecological integrity in landscapes have always been largely intuitive, so have perceptions of form in art. Mature forests provide esthetic pleasure

to millions who know nothing about the processes of ecological balance which maintain them. Only recently has
ecology developed the necessary techniques for describing
the processes which govern ecosystem integrity. Similarly,
readers have been pleased for many centuries by Homer's
Iliad without perceiving the intricate structural relationships of its component elements, and few who respond to a
Bach fugue are capable of comprehending the principles of
its rhythmic and harmonic balance. Whether audiences
understand such intricacies or not, they respond to them
esthetically. Greater analytical knowledge merely increases
the sense of awe and wonder at the contemplation of natural
and artistic systems, whether they are understood as biologists do or as art critics do.

The principle of ecological integrity is *internal* to the
pleasing landscape or work of art and is not only a projec-
tion of human desires or expectations. When someone calls
a landscape beautiful, thus affirming that its excellence is
subjectively valuable, what he is really seeing is the result
of natural processes which have proceeded for millennia
without any concern for human satisfactions. Beautiful
landscapes do not exist for human enjoyment, nor do they
communicate the ideas of some Great Ecologist in the Sky.
In their egotistic way, humans have often assumed that
natural beauty must be a message from an Artist-God, thus
fusing (or confusing) biological and metaphysical reality
into a grand pantheistic whole.

When people experience a great work of art they sometimes assume that the artist is trying to tell them something,
and elaborate systems have been created for interpreting
the "message" of Dante, Shakespeare, or Beethoven. But
great works of art are not devices for communication be-

tween an artist and his public any more than ecosystems are messages from a creator. Both depend upon internal systems of balance which constitute a self-sustaining equilibrium of multiple elements. Neither depends upon its ability to teach humans or to change their lives.

But certainly humans can learn from both, providing that the right kinds of questions are asked. Too often critics and biologists have applied simplistic criteria to their interpretations of nature and art. The preoccupation with a man-centered ethical tradition has led theorists to apply standards of good and evil without being aware of the distortions thus created. A wolf may look villainous to a sheep rancher, but only so long as he fails to see the importance of predation to the maintenance of long-term environmental stability. Similarly, audiences may hate Iago and admire Othello without recognizing that the structure of Shakespeare's play depends equally upon both characters. The predation of wolves and Iagos is essential to the systems they respectively belong to. If the rancher succeeds in destroying wolves he has weakened the integrity of the ecosystem upon which his own life ultimately depends. And when Othello allows himself to be misled by Iago, he tragically destroys the innocent Desdemona, the political stability of his community, and himself. The search for villains and heroes in either case by applying simple moral judgments is sure to do violence to the natural and artistic systems under study. Ranchers and Othellos become tragic when they destructively fail to respond to the complexities of their own environments. Western man need no longer follow such examples.

Neither art nor nature can affirm that creation is better than destruction, but both offer understanding of how the two forces relate to one another in a given context. To study ecology and to study literature it is necessary to concentrate on the processes and relationships which govern the interactions of ideas, creatures, and environment. The study of process does not yield information about good or evil, but it can tell something about causes and consequences, growth and decay, stability and chaos.

Evolution and ecological succession tend toward maximum diversity of form and function. Ecological development proceeds from a pioneer stage toward higher successional levels, creating an ever more complex and stable environment at each stage. The numbers of specialized species increase, as do the relationships among them, until an advanced stage is reached in which the maximum plant and animal population for a given geographic setting has been reached. A stable ecosystem, however, is not the end of a process, nor is it a static state. Rather, it is a homeostatic system where growth and decay are in equilibrium, and where the needs and activities of every species are accommodated, including predation and the normal death and destruction necessary for the maintenance of life. Maximum complexity and diversity are essential to the maximum durability of the system as a whole.

The tendency toward intricate balance in ecosystems is a feature of biological evolution as well. Darwin's account of the origin of species and more than a century of research in its wake have resulted in a rather detailed picture of the evolutionary movement toward ever greater diversity. The two models of biological reality, the ecological and the evolutionary, present images of life as a process. If there is a scale of ethical values implied in this model, it rests upon the supposition that complexity is better than simplicity merely because it is more adaptable to change and therefore more durable. And if a scale of esthetic values is implied, it seems clear that the human sense of beauty is increasingly satisfied at each advancing stage of successional diversity.

Artistic Ecology and Ecological Art

It is important to remember that both ecology and art are models of reality invented by humans. They are the products of consciousness and of the talent for creating abstractions which seem to be peculiar to our species. Neither the simple hippopotamus nor the sophisticated dolphin is aware of the intricate ecological processes of which his private existence is a small part. Even the human mind can grasp such conceptions only in a halting and incomplete manner. However deeply animals may be immersed in their ecosystems, man is the only animal capable of describing how such systems work. The same mental capacity makes it possible for man to modify ecosystems, often to their destruction, and to create such systems as an act of the imagination. The human mentality gives mankind the power to create imaginary ecosystems (as has been done in art), to destroy them (as has been done with technology), and to explain them (as man is beginning to do with scientific ecology). The similarities between esthetic and ecological conceptions of nature suggest the possibility that the two may reinforce each other in the effort to change the long history of destruction our species has caused by its simplistic view of nature. A common ground exists between art and ecology which may help to end the long strife between thought and intuition, science and art, and possibly even that between man and nature.

Impediments to such a hopeful prospect are many, but

chief among them may be the intellectual biases which often prevent scientists and humanists from talking intelligibly to one another. Even when an honest attempt is made to cross disciplinary boundaries, people tend to drag along their old suppositions, perhaps without even knowing it. Thus Professor Weiss, a biologist, finds that art affirms what he has previously discovered in the scientific laboratory, and Professor Langer, a philosopher, finds in biology an apt metaphor to illustrate her prior interest in human emotions. Since both arguments are brilliant and convincing, readers are likely to be confused by their different conclusions: does beauty lie in the order inherent in things, as Weiss insists, or in the expression of human emotion, as Langer insists? Is it "in" the things to which we respond esthetically, or is it a quality which we bring to them?

It has been said that if a mixed group of scientists and humanists were asked to investigate a report of an angel floating in the sky nearby, the scientists would at once go to the spot and invent experiments to determine whether an angel was in fact present or not, while the humanists would examine the motives and state of mind of the witness who claimed to have seen the angel. If the angel in question is esthetic experience, Professors Weiss and Langer fill the roles of scientists and humanists respectively, illustrating the traditionally separate products of "objectivity" and "subjectivity." The scientist tends to forget that both order and beauty are abstract concepts invented by man, and the humanist often forgets that man is as much a part of nature as the system to which he responds.

Without pursuing the endless intricacies of argument between the two approaches, it is worthwhile to point out that their separation no longer seems either necessary or appropriate. The human experience of beauty is rooted in natural forms and processes which exist with or without human perception, and our esthetic values are really no more—nor any less—than abstract formulations of the natural as it exists both within us and around us. What is exclusively human is generally not beautiful to us, and we find beauty in human art only when it is compatible with forms and processes in nature. The humanist's interest in emotions and ideas can never be satisfied except through greater knowledge of the natural world of which ideas and emotions are themselves a biological part. And the scientists must know, if they are honest with themselves, that subjective and emotional experiences are among the important elements of objective reality. Scientists must also recognize in candor that their interpretations represent models of reality, not reality itself. A good scientific theory or paradigm is as imaginative a creation as a good work of art, except perhaps that a work of art is likely to last longer since it is less subject to contradiction.

The emergence of ecology as a potent new model of reality offers an unprecedented opportunity to reconcile the products of humanistic and scientific investigation. Their separation, in fact, becomes absurd once it is accepted that man and his works are elements in a world ecosphere and when it is recognized that natural processes have provided the basic forms for human thought and creativity. Ecology demonstrates the interpenetrability of man and the natural environment, an insight which is richly confirmed by the evidence of human artistic creations.

SEVEN

Ingredients for an Environmental Ethic

WILLIAM FAULKNER LIKED TO REPEAT A CHINESE FABLE about a time when cats were the dominant creatures on earth. After centuries of failure in their attempts to solve the ethical problems faced by a dominant species, the cat philosophers decided that the only practical solution was to give it up and to select from the lesser creatures some species that would be "optimistic enough to believe that the mortal predicament could be solved and ignorant enough never to learn better." According to the narrator in *The Reivers,* "that is why the cat lives with you, is completely dependent on you for food and shelter, but lifts no paw for you and loves you not; in a word, why your cat looks at you the way it does." [1] Humans have persisted, optimistically and ignorantly, in their belief that ethical problems can be solved, disregarding several thousand years' accumulation of evidence to the contrary. Though our species may not yet be ready to follow the cats' example by abdicating in favor of some other species, we might be wise to pay some attention to those animals whose behavior and environmental relationships can teach us something about our own.

People have often used animals to illustrate minor truths about social behavior in children's stories and moral fables, but they seldom take animals seriously as sources of philosophical insight into human ethics. Westerners, at least, have preferred to believe that ethical law comes from outside the world of matter, nature, and experience. The biblical image of Moses on his mountaintop receiving the tables of the law from an extraterrestrial God is typical. So is Plato's analogy of the cave in *The Republic*, where ideas of good and evil are shown to be beyond sense perception and far above the environment of life in a realm that the Greeks called *meta-physical*, beyond existence. The assumption that ethical principles are supra-environmental in origin is one of the strongest legacies of Western thought. Though its ancient Hebrew and Greek forms may have lost credit in recent centuries, it persists in modern fantasies about superior beings from outer space and in religious conceptions of a Power which regulates experience from some Beyond.

It has become possible in this century to consider the development of a true environmental ethic based upon the human experience of events in the world, upon the evolutionary history of the human and other species, and upon the new knowledge of ecological principles which govern the relationships of organisms to their natural environments. Such an ethic must emphasize the survival of the species rather than spiritual salvation or transcendence, and its methods must provide for adaptation to the natural environment rather than conquest of it.

Environmental ethics must confront two large problems: humans' relationships to other humans (intraspecific ethics), and humans' relationships to the plants and animals of the natural environment (interspecific ethics). Ethology offers insight into the first, and ecology into the second.

THE ETHOLOGY OF INTRASPECIFIC BEHAVIOR

The relationship between animal and human behavior is not merely one of analogy. Men are not only *like* animals, they *are* animals, and the recognition of man as an animal does not simplify or reduce man's stature in the least.

The study of wild animal behavior has become scientifically respectable only within the past few decades. Biology no longer need limit itself to the study of anatomy and physiology, but has now begun to perfect the interdisciplinary techniques of ecology and ethology as legitimate scientific inquiries. These are the first biological approaches which hold promise of revealing new knowledge about the complex interrelationships which govern organic life in all its forms. Their purpose is to see the various forms of life in context with one another, not in isolation. This context, of course, also includes the life form that we call humanity.

These two new features of biological thought—the recognition that man is an animal and the development of techniques for the study of all animal relationships and behavior—have now made it possible to begin disassembling the barrier wall that has separated the world of man from the world of nature. So far, only a little has been learned about the common denominators of human and animal ethical behavior. But already there is enough evidence to justify the hope that an ethical continuum may one day emerge showing man as an integrated part of nature rather than a unique exception.

Sex

Sexual behavior seems to be highest on most people's lists of biological interests, perhaps because people have been most confused about this aspect of moral behavior. The pair bond—known as marriage in the human ethical tradition— is not a uniquely human invention, but is practiced by many other species, some of which make it work much better than humans do. Among "marrying" animals, such as wolves and geese, fidelity is often assured simply because all extramarital sexual interests disappear permanently when the pair bond is formed. The mated pair is a permanent family unit dedicated to the rearing of young and the defense of its territory, and it normally survives competitive sexual enticements or even the death of one of the partners. As the American sexologist A. C. Kinsey and many others have demonstrated, human attempts to enforce the family bond by ethical laws and customs have not been nearly so successful. For six millennia civil and religious laws have forbidden men from coveting their neighbors' wives, yet they covet nonetheless. Humans seem to hanker for sexual variety no matter how much they believe that they shouldn't.

On the other hand, the happy promiscuity of many primate species, such as baboons and howling monkeys, seems unsuited to human needs, however great its playboy attractions may be. Since human offspring require so many years to mature, there seems to be a need for the permanent family security that only the pair bond can assure. Other mating arrangements, such as free love or polygamy, have never proved very satisfying or satisfactory to people, though several other animal species have made them work rather well.

After thousands of years of sexual discomfort, we remain unhappily in ignorance and guilt concerning our own most appropriate mating behavior. This confusion may result from the moralizing attempts made by civilization to repress and control human instinctual sexual needs. We have generally used our superior mental ability to suppress—rather than to fulfill—our sexual instincts, and the cost has generally been paid in neurosis. If we were to devote our efforts to discovering what the sexual and mating needs of our species in fact *are,* rather than trying to enforce what we think they *should* be, perhaps we would begin to discover forms of sexual behavior that would both satisfy us and assure the successful survival of our kind, as other species have done.

Ownership and Social Organization

Territorial rights are as important among animals as they are among men. Animals are attached to their land, and they form themselves into social groups which provide internal security and defense against intrusion. Many patterns of social and territorial behavior exist among animals. Each territorial species has its own form of territorial and social organization which suits its particular needs and enhances its opportunities for biological success.

Some species have a high degree of individuation in a social organization that fosters strong authoritarian leadership. Others emphasize internal cooperation, distribution of power among members of the group, and concerted self-less action in the defense of territory. Human social organization is not a uniquely human invention, but the product of evolutionary influences similar to those which have governed the development of other animal societies.

But again the question arises, is there a form of social organization which answers most effectively to the needs of the human species? The enlarged human brain has long exerted itself to create utopian societies designed to achieve human perfection, and nowhere have humans caused themselves more pain and destruction than in these efforts. We have tried everything our mentality and imagination can devise, but we have not yet tried to assess the complicated social needs of man as a biological species.

Aggression

Perhaps the most pressing need today is to learn more about human aggressive behavior. The human race has the capacity to render itself extinct unless alternatives are found to the patterns of intraspecific warfare that have dominated civilized history. Ours has long been a predatory species. Living, for humans, depends upon the ability to kill as clearly as it does for lions or wolves. But lions and wolves, like almost all predatory species, normally limit their killing to prey animals, and they are equipped with elaborate ritual precautions to prevent the destruction of their own kind. Humans appear to be unique among predators in their enthusiasm to destroy members of their own species. Perhaps this unusual behavior can be attributed to some genetic deficiency which may lead humans ultimately to join the rest of nature's failures in the biological graveyard of extinction. Or perhaps our willingness to kill ourselves, like so many of our other problems, is something we have devised by misusing our enlarged brains.

Predatory animals act according to two different patterns of aggressive behavior which appear to be governed by separate neural substrates in the brain. One kind of aggression is designed to kill animals of another species for food. The death of another animal is the sole object of this behavioral pattern, and it is of course necessary to the survival of any meat-eating predator. But such killing behavior is virtually never directed against another member of the predator's own species. Aggression among members of the same species serves a social, not a nutritional, purpose. Intraspecific aggression establishes the relative social status of animals as they relate to one another in families and social groups, and rarely results in death. Predatory ethics *require* that animals of other species be killed, and at the same time *forbid* that members of one's own species be killed.

Human ethical traditions generally agree with that distinction, though we seem to have found many ways of behaving which contradict it: warfare, legal death penalties, and murders of infinite variety. Our justifications for killing other human beings all seem to derive from the rational human mind, not from our genetic heritage. We have invented schemes which permit us to treat other humans as if they were members of another species—rats, dogs, snakes, pigs—as if we could deceive ourselves into believing that their murder was therefore proper. As noted in the discussion of *Hamlet,* it is much easier to kill another human if he is identified as a beast, not a human. Other predatory animals have been unable to create such illusions because they lack our complex brain, so they kill other species only in order to eat, and fight with members of their own species without killing. Humans would be wise to study that distinction.

The Ethics of the Species

The human animal, like all other animals, has its own specific pattern of behavior. There is no more wisdom in judging humans according to the behavior of chimpanzees than there would be in judging gorillas or wolves by the same standards, and all analogies are likely to be misleading.

A concerted attempt must be made to discover the basic patterns of behavior that are peculiar to the phylogeny of the human species. To accomplish this, it will be necessary to sort out the instinctual patterns of human behavior from the cultural overlays and contradictions that civilization has deposited upon them. As Konrad Lorenz has said, "Man is by nature a creature of culture"—that is, civilized human culture is now an integral part of the biological evolution of our species. Our culture is also the most quickly adaptable of all our features, providing we can decide in which direction we want to go. We must find a way to distinguish between those cultural ideas which seek to repress or destroy our instinctual needs and those which seek to fulfill them. This is a task we have never before been in a position to undertake, and it will not be an easy one to achieve.

The present sciences of human behavior—sociology, psychology, anthropology—have scarcely addressed themselves to this problem; they seem to be preoccupied with the environmental determinants of human ontogeny and have largely overlooked the phylogenetic implications of evolutionary biology. Psychology took an evolutionary view of human behavior under Freud and Jung (when very little knowledge of animal behavior was available), but has since seemed more interested in the study of human cultural environments as the sole sources of psychic and social life. Philosophy has devoted itself mostly to the study of symbolic logic. So the most provocative new ideas in ethical thought in our time have come from an unexpected source: ecological biology. It is biology that seems most likely to show us how to study man as he is: his origins, the phylogenetic sources of his behavior, and his role in the economy of nature.

An important step toward reconciling human phylogeny with human culture was taken by the contemporary American ecologist Paul Shepard in *The Tender Carnivore and the Sacred Game.*[2] Humane life did not begin with the invention of agriculture and the domestication of animals, Shepard points out, but may have ended then. When men and women gave up hunting and gathering and began to manipulate natural processes for strictly human ends some eight thousand years ago, they took the first steps toward destruction of the earth's ecology and cut themselves off from their evolutionary past. Mankind thus sacrificed an ecologically oriented way of life that had taken a million years to develop and gained in exchange the power to disrupt the world and to manufacture widespread human unhappiness.

With agriculture came the beginnings of population growth, soil erosion and depletion, the extinction of wild animal species, and the waste of mineral and natural resources—all of which have nearly achieved perfection in our time as components of environmental crisis. The political and ideological values fostered by agriculture added tyranny, acquisitiveness, boredom, the exploitation of women, and the invention of warfare to the human repertoire, and created the cultural climate from which the modern industrial state was to grow with its cities full of unfulfilled human beings.

The hunting-gathering culture which agriculture replaced, Shepard argues, was not at all as brutish and miserable as depicted in popular anthropology. Hunting man lived finely tuned to his surroundings, healthy and alert of mind and body, with his numbers and his social structure regulated to his environment. Moreover, his religion and his highly sophisticated art forms were cultural bonds which enhanced his sense of unity with his fellow humans and with the animals and plants upon which his life depended.

Shepard builds his description of hunting life upon current anthropological evidence and upon recent discoveries in primate evolution and ethology. In search of "the ecology native to our species," Shepard summarizes and interprets the new knowledge of primate behavior and human anthropology which has become available only in the past decade. Patterns of basic human biology and the behavior appropriate to them emerge from his careful analyses of Paleolithic life and art, of modern hunting-gathering peoples, and of the remarkable evolutionary heredity of the carnivorous primates which we all are.

Paul Shepard's *Tender Carnivore* addresses itself to essential issues which cannot be ignored. The further exploration of these issues will likely lead to an ethical reappraisal of human culture.

Ethical Bankruptcy

It is common to hear that the Western ethical tradition is bankrupt. Nietzsche made the point very effectively almost a century ago, and existential philosophy has since accomplished a rather thorough accounting of our moral poverty. In an essay by the modern French existentialist philosopher Jean-Paul Sartre, the human predicament is symbolized with wonderful clarity and simplicity. Sartre tells the story of a young French student in 1940 who had to make a choice between staying with his mother, who needed his help to survive during the war, and serving his country by joining the Free French Forces. Sartre examines the entire bulk of ethical tradition from Christian morality through Kant's categorical imperative and is unable to find an applicable moral principle on which the young man can base his decision. He concludes that "no rule of general morality can show you what you ought to do," and so he advises the boy: "You are free, therefore choose." [3] Sartre's point is that man is "condemned to be free," that the traditions of moral behavior inherited from our civilized past provide no dependable guidance for behavior, and so humans must invent their morality as best they can in particular circumstances.

While agreeing with Sartre's judgment of our inadequate tradition of philosophical ethics, I would add that this young man's problem was also *created* by the same ethical philosophy that failed to solve it. The young man's choice seems difficult only because he has been taught that such an abstract concept as "France" really exists. The concept of a nation is a mental construct for which there is no genuine biological counterpart. The relationship between mother and child, however, is one of the world's strongest bonds because it is firmly rooted in both instinct and experience for all of us—and for most other mammals as well. A million years of evolution went into the development of that young man's bond to his mother; the ideas of "nation" and "patriotism" are only a few hundred years old, and can hardly compete with the mother-child relationship unless we happen to be as morally confused as Sartre's young friend was.

Similar instinctive bonds tie us to our friends. The British novelist E. M. Forster put it directly and accurately: "If I had to choose between betraying my country and betraying my friend, I hope I should have the guts to betray my country."[4] Forster's choice rests upon the deep emotional attachments to individual persons derived from the evolutionary history of the human species and confirmed by recent observations among other animals as well. As an ethical posture, it is millions of years old. Friends are more real than nations.

Alyosha's Choice

Perhaps the clearest illustration of this theme is to be found in Fyodor Dostoyevsky's great Russian novel of the late nineteenth century, *The Brothers Karamazov*. Just before the famous "Grand Inquisitor" chapter, midway through the novel, Dostoyevsky presents a discussion between Ivan, the intellectual idealist in the novel, and Alyosha, who is Dostoyevsky's version of what Jesus might be like if he were living in the modern world. Ivan offers Alyosha a hypothetical choice: Suppose you were given the power, he says, to create a perfect human world in which mankind would be happy and peaceful and all human needs would be satisfied, but in order to do that you would have to begin by torturing to death one innocent child. Would you take the job on that condition? [5]

This is a basic ethical choice between the welfare of all humanity and the suffering of one helpless child. Certainly the child's death would be a moral crime, yet when it is weighed against the welfare of mankind it seems a small price to pay. From Plato through Thomas Jefferson or Karl Marx (whichever you prefer), ethical tradition has placed the welfare and brotherhood of mankind above all private suffering. The most respected humanistic values would be realizable if Alyosha agreed to kill the child in order to create the perfect human society.

Yet Alyosha, the Christ figure, rejects the thought of torturing a child, whatever good might come of it for society. He is hard pressed to explain his choice, and finally takes refuge in Christian doctrine which says that justice is in the hands of God, not man. His answer fails to explain *why* it is ethically unacceptable to him to build a good society beginning with an evil act. Most people agree with Alyosha, but it is not easy to explain why. Ivan's offer makes sense and Alyosha's rejection doesn't. Ivan affirms humanitarian ideals that most people believe in, and Alyosha is an archaic Christian saint whose beliefs few today can share. It is not merely Dostoyevsky's subtle artistry that puts most people on Alyosha's side, but something much deeper.

People may agree with Alyosha because he affirms an innate prohibition against the murder of a child. That prohibition is deeply rooted in phylogenetic origins and is not merely a moral doctrine to which people have given their conscious assent. Most people would be at a loss to explain it rationally, just as Alyosha is. But an examination of other primates—and of many other animals as well—shows that they exhibit the same solicitude for young members of their own species. Few innate patterns of behavior are stronger than those commanding that young mammals may not become objects of aggression, but must be protected against such dangers, whatever the cost.

Ivan's proposal for the good of humanity, on the other hand, is a thoroughly civilized notion. His ideas of human perfectibility, of dignity and honor, of justice and logic, all presuppose the history of human consciousness from which they are derived. These concepts originated with Greek classical philosophy, and are at most three thousand years old. They are abstract formulations of rational human thought which people can accept or reject according to their own cultural backgrounds and intellectual preferences. None of them can be clearly confirmed by reference to our primate ancestors or to other animals.

Dostoyevsky's ethical problem thus looks like a conflict between Western idealism and innate human emotional behavior. Intellectually and rationally, it is easy to appreciate the wisdom of sacrificing an innocent child in order to attain the happiness of all humanity. Emotionally, "all humanity" is meaningless to humans and is decidedly subordinate to our concern for the safety of the child. Only a fanatically dedicated idealist would use his mind to justify acting in contradiction to such powerful innate human emotions. Dostoyevsky's novel is about people who use their minds in that way and destroy themselves and others in the process.

Domesticated Ethics

It is possible to disrupt the normal ethical behavior of an animal species by imposing special conditions and restraints, either mental or environmental. When humans domesticate animals we change their ethical behavior, just as we change their physical features, by selectively breeding for behavioral traits which will be convenient to human purposes. Normal killing or food-gathering behavior and defensive aggression are suppressed when wild animals are domesticated, patterns of courtship and mating behavior are destroyed, and a premium is placed upon those animals who will breed promiscuously at the farmer's will without time wasted in ritual mating ceremonies or battles fought among males to earn the right to mate. Domestic animals are bred for minimum aggression and maximum submissiveness, which generally means that they never reach normal stages of maturity for their species. Domestication weakens the intraspecific bonds among animals, subverts normal social structures, and destroys the animals' usual relationships to their natural environments.

The domestication of animals attacks those patterns of ethical behavior which human moral philosophy has often admired: sexual selectivity and fidelity, social order consistent with individual liberty, the skills of self-support, defensive strength against attack, and strong social leadership. If domesticated animals appear to be "beastly," it is often because domestication has made them so.

To a certain extent, mankind itself may be regarded as a domesticated species. The power of civilization may have suppressed certain instinctual patterns of behavior which protected the chances for survival of our species. Civilized morality has tried hard to control certain basic patterns of human behavior, especially those relating to sexuality and aggression. The contemporary breakdown of many traditional ethical patterns long fostered by human culture may be a disaster for our species, as some think, or it may be the beginning of a liberation from some of the restraints of self-domestication. There is certainly a need to find ethical principles and practices which will agree better with the biological requirements of the human species and which will serve the interest of human survival. The prospects may depend upon how much can be learned in the near future about the behavior of the animals around us and the animal that is within us.

INTERSPECIFIC ETHICS

In both the Greek and the Judeo-Christian tradition, the world is believed to exist in order to be useful to mankind. Man is assumed to enjoy special privileges over nature but to bear almost no ethical responsibilities for maintaining natural processes. Mankind has gloried in its ability to bend and shape the world to suit human interests but has shown little concern for shaping human behavior toward greater compatibility with the natural environment.

The Western ethical tradition has been humanistic and theological, not environmental. Changes are now occurring in this old pattern, and not merely since ecology has achieved some public notice. Quite apart from the social movements which have responded lately to environmental crisis, ethical thinking for the past few centuries has moved ever closer to the natural world as a source of ethical guidance. A new environmental ethic has been in the making for several centuries, and the current environmental crisis has helped to hasten its development.

The Death of God

Traditional models of reality have been subjected to scathing critiques during the past four centuries. Religion has perhaps suffered most, or at least most obviously. The twins born of the Renaissance, modern humanism and inductive science, proved apostate to religion because they insisted that man and this physical world are the only legitimate human concerns, and that both are essentially subject to human control without need for divine assistance. Once those views had been established, it was inevitable that a Nietzsche would appear to announce the death of God. Since Nietzsche, demolition of the ancient religious edifice has proceeded rapidly under the blows of existentialism and with the generous cooperation of scientific and economic materialism. The resulting rubble is both God's tombstone and a monument to the divinity of man. As Dostoyevsky's character Kirilov puts it in *The Devils:* "If there is no God then I am a God." [6] Man took the place of his dead god.

Another of Dostoyevsky's characters, Ivan Karamazov, anticipates Nietzsche with a similarly provocative syllogism: *If there is no God, then everything is permitted.*[7] When faith in an ordering deity was rejected, so was faith in the systems of moral and social law which had been built largely upon religious foundations. The vacuum left by the disappearance of divine ethical standards and goals has yet to be filled by any of the systems that have competed for allegiance during the past century—nationalism, communism, industrialism, individualism, aestheticism, escapism, and a host of lesser persuasions—even though each offers its followers a substantial guide to social and ethical behavior. These ideologies have tended to exclude one another, each one insisting upon its own principles, none catholic enough to replace Catholicism, none persuasive enough to capture man's imagination as religions once did.

Modern technology has been for many the clearest sign of man's divinity. Since Leonardo da Vinci dreamed early in the sixteenth century of damming rivers and flying through the air, engineers have shared and compounded his vision even beyond Leonardo's outlandish schemes. The technological West has lately all but freed humanity from the dangers and inconveniences of natural existence—or at least has created the illusion of this freedom. Clever man seems to have provided for himself better than God could, and man accordingly deserves worship. The worship of industrial technology has thus become a new humanistic religion professed by many scientists, politicians, businessmen, and ordinary citizens for whom no other kind of religious belief is possible.

Unfortunately, the adoration of technological man has led to serious damage of our biological environment. Its ideology has also weakened irreparably our faith in traditional philosophical and religious values. Both body and soul, we are cut off from systems of order which have sustained us in the past, so it is little wonder that mankind feels badly equipped for the future.

The Paradoxes of Utilitarian Ethics

Utilitarian ethical systems assume that the results of human action are predictable and can be weighed in advance against several alternatives. The utilitarian ideology behind the "Green Revolution," the recent attempt by Western agricultural technology to increase food harvests in "have not" nations, assumes that it is "good" to provide food for starving human populations in developing nations, and "good" to create new foreign markets for American chemicals and agricultural technology—and that both of these results will follow from the application of highly technological agriculture in developing nations. It assumes that many human advantages will accompany the more efficient exploitation of agricultural land, and that humanity will, on the whole, be happier and more peaceful thanks to an increased food supply. There may be some unfortunate side effects—such as loss of wildlife habitat, loss of genetic diversity among food crops, changes in the cultural traditions associated with Oriental agriculture, and the disruption of the economic and political systems of the countries affected by their dependency upon complex technologies—but these are considered minor sacrifices compared to the greater goods that will predictably be accomplished in the interest of human dignity and relief from starvation. This is a bit like sacrificing a child in order to attain a perfect society.

Most Americans find this utilitarian argument very convincing; they have heard and accepted it all their lives. Such concepts of "the greater good" justified our great-grandfathers' appropriation by force and by stealth of the lands of American Indians, on the assumption that the Indians were using the land less efficiently than white men could. We have similarly justified the damming of our rivers, the extinction of many animal species ("pests and predators"), the introduction of chemical pesticides and fertilizers, the development of highway and airline systems, the encouragement of mineral exploitation, and urban industrial development.

The utilitarian argument recurs daily in debates over such projects as oil pipelines and generating plants, where the "tradeoffs" among good and bad results of such projects are weighed, or a cost-benefit analysis is made which will predict the results of technological activities. The predictions made by such systems of analysis, of course, have generally been confirmed by subsequent events. Engineers' expectations of the positive effects of technology have regularly proved to be correct. The problem is that these developments have also created *other* effects which were not, and could not be, predicted.

An impressive list of "benefactors of humanity" according to utilitarian principles can be compiled from the records of the Nobel Prizes and the many other rewards bestowed upon those who have discovered new ways to serve human health and happiness. But a close look at that list will also reveal that it identifies the source of many discoveries which have threatened the continuation of life: such things as atomic energy, the endless growth techniques of economics, DDT, genetic controls over organic life, the medical breakthroughs which have encouraged population explosion, and now the Green Revolution.

All these creative inventions were motivated by the desire to make the world a better place to live in and to increase human welfare and dignity. Although the predicted effects have often been achieved, the record is still dismal, largely because each of these "advances" has had many consequences which could not have been anticipated in advance. A dedicated servant of humanity like Louis Pasteur could never have predicted that his founding of the science of bacteriology, by helping to increase human population growth, would lead toward greater human suffering than medical technology could possibly alleviate. Many of the atomic scientists who invented a bomb to end the bloodshed of World War II were appalled at the political, social, and psychological disruptions that have created near chaos in the atomic age. No one can predict the widespread results likely to follow from such unprecedented services to humanity as the Green Revolution or a cure for cancer. Utilitarian science "in the service of humanity" is wonderfully successful, but each of its successes seems to have produced new and unexpected threats to life. The experience of the past four hundred years of Western history suggests that man's most energetic efforts to achieve the good life have also robbed life of much of the meaning that less inventive, less idealistic humans have found in it.

The Imperfectibility of Man

Utilitarian philosophy is built upon a faith that human beings are perfectible and that they will grow in goodness as they are released from bondage to nature by an increasingly efficient technology. As machines perform their tasks ever more perfectly, mankind is expected to use the resulting leisure and freedom to cultivate reason, goodness, and beauty. As machines become more *mechanically* efficient, humans should grow more *ethically* efficient, gaining in wisdom, judgment, and compassion according to the degree of their relief from drudgery and fear.

There is little evidence from recent history to support such predictions. Rather, an opposite result seems to have followed. We are coming to think of ourselves much as we think of the machines that were supposed to liberate us. We look increasingly to elaborate laws and legislative programs to solve human problems, and to education and the public media to produce desirable mental states on a large scale. We tinker with social structures and human consciousness as if they were complicated computers which will surely produce the right answers if only we learn how to program them properly. Absorbed as we are in this task, it is easy to overlook how miserable many individual lives are, or how gross our ethical sensibilities have become. Side by side with our visions of a perfected humanity are such modern events as ten years of meaningless destruction in Southeast Asia, Hitler's murder of six million Jews, the wholesale extinction of many animal species, the pollution of land, sea, and air on a worldwide basis, and the many lesser instances of human crime and moral degradation which punctuate our newspapers and motion pictures, all reminders that there are millions of neurotic and morally confused human beings who suffer somewhere in the hidden crannies of our shiny social machine.

Stuart Hampshire, a British philosopher at Cambridge University, has offered a critique of utilitarian morality which identifies its fundamental flaw. Utilitarian ethics, he says, teach that humans can and ought to use and exploit each other just as they use and exploit any other natural objects. The utilitarian ethic teaches that the techniques for exploiting and manipulating nature are applicable to the exploitation and manipulation of mankind as well. What utilitarianism failed to predict, however, is that both nature and humanity are subject to degradation and pollution by these same techniques. We have corrupted ourselves by the same methods we have used to corrupt the processes of nature.

Hampshire's penetrating essay concludes with a simple and sobering judgment which some may find pessimistic: "Moral progress . . . is not to be expected except within very narrow limits." The utilitarians since Jeremy Bentham and John Stuart Mill have "looked for an historical transformation of human nature through new moral reasoning, [but] this has not occurred and is now not to be reasonably expected." [8] The utilitarian dream of a conquered nature and a perfected humanity must take its place among the many other idealistic fantasies which have produced disappointing and destructive consequences.

Evolution's Revelation

If Hampshire is right, what alternatives are left for ethical guidance that will better meet both human needs and the requirements of a healthy natural environment? One genuinely creative moment of intellectual history occurred a century ago with Darwin's articulation of the principles of evolution by natural selection. As materialism and atheism barred us from God, evolution introduced us to our nearer neighbors, plants and animals. The recognition that we are animals lets us look upon ourselves not as divinity or superman, but as an organic participant in a natural world, and as a species with an appropriate situation in the natural environment. Since Darwin, natural history and the increasingly sophisticated disciplines that have emerged from it, especially modern ecology, have revealed an intricate panorama of natural relationships and interdependencies. The spectacle was always under our noses, but it had escaped our notice while we were gazing at the stars or at our own flattering image in a highly polished technological mirror.

One sure consequence of ecology is already apparent: the complexity of our thinking about the world must increase to accommodate orders of intricacy which we have never before imagined. We have grossly oversimplified the world in our belief that we were the only important creatures in it. Yet the dangers of zoomorphizing man are as great as those of anthropomorphizing or even ignoring nature. Man's capacity for symbolic and abstract thought does set us apart from other animals, though we frequently exaggerate that difference or mistake its significance. The study of man must deal with him not only as an animal but also as one with a unique capacity for manipulating his habitat, for comprehending his environment, and for undertaking distinctively human imaginative and spiritual experiences. Whether it fosters pride or despair, the mind inescapably dominates both the acts that will shape human survival and the durability of the ecological environment upon which all life depends.

It is generally assumed that the human mind is capable of evolutionary growth, that it can adapt itself to cope with any environmental changes so as to improve the prospects of man's survival within a stable biosphere. This assumption is not necessarily correct. Many species' specialized organs apparently have become maladaptive under transformed environmental circumstances and thus have contributed to the species' extinction. To assume a priori that the brain insures evolutionary "privilege" on into an indeterminate future is to indulge a biological complacency that is both perilous and thoughtless.

Man's fate over the long, evolutionary haul, as much as from day to day, will be determined by what happens in the human mind and in its collective product, cultural history.

The best prospect for this species lies in the adaptability of human mental activities, not of bodily processes. The hope of survival lies in the human talent for rapid adaptive mental change, but changes in human mentality customarily proceed at a glacial pace. Several centuries often intervene between the appearance of new ideas and the cultural and intellectual changes appropriate to them. Although improved communications seem to have greatly accelerated this process since the Renaissance, substantial agents of lag still exist. For example, the dissemination of new ideas is often controlled by those who most resist evolutionary change. Further, the virtually unmanageable array of demands upon the human mind results in as much perplexity and irresolution as it does in revision. Most ironically, the very flexibility of the mind often leads not to adaptive clarity and decision but rather to confusion, as we broad-mindedly examine so many sides of a question that we find ourselves unable to sort out the resulting intellectual contradictions. Many are in such a state now about "ecology," frustrated by their inability to choose at a time when critical questions must be answered: What out of our past is pertinent? What in our predicament is even within our means to change? The guidelines of sustained coherent thought, let alone decision, seem indecipherable. But then, we have barely begun.

Adaptive Intelligence

Humans properly take pride in human intelligence, and they have customarily expected the intellect to solve ethical problems. This is a reasonable expectation only if our intelligence is used differently from the way it generally has been in the past. William Faulkner's picaresque definition of intelligence is worth reviewing: *"the ability to cope with environment: which means to accept environment yet still retain at least something of personal liberty."* [9] Intelligence is not merely the ability to be trained, or to comprehend abstract symbolisms, or to invent tools and technologies, or to manipulate the world for human advantage. It is a measure of the ability to understand the conditions of the environment into which one has been accidentally born, to accept those conditions, and to adapt oneself to them.

An environmental ethic requires that human behavior be modified to agree with the ecology of the world, not that the world be rearranged to suit human desires. The appropriate changes will not mean a simplification of human life but far greater complexity, both in human life and in the diversity of plants and animals with which we share the natural environment, than has been known in the past. Human beings must learn more about what the world is really like and spend less time dreaming about how they would like it to be if they could change it.

Adaptation to environment is more than just a defensive technique of survival in an endangered circumstance. It is a creative ethic which requires that all scientific and imaginative powers be directed toward encouraging a more durable equilibrium among the various forms of life. It is the principle which might well provide the foundation for a new and imaginative environmental ethic, as it did for Mann's Felix Krull: "He who really loves the world shapes himself to please it." [10] With luck and some imagination, perhaps the human race can do better than those Chinese cats who gave up and left their problems for some other species to solve.

EIGHT

The Comedy of Dante's *Comedy*

Dᴀɴᴛᴇ ᴀʟɪɢʜɪᴇʀɪ, ᴛʜᴇ ғᴏᴜʀᴛᴇᴇɴᴛʜ-ᴄᴇɴᴛᴜʀʏ ɪᴛᴀʟɪᴀɴ poet, called his great poem simply the *Comedy*. Some theologians who mistook Dante's intention later added *Divine*, and the mistake has led readers since to see the work as a textbook of medieval religious beliefs. But Dante's purpose was "to remove those living in this life from the state of misery and lead them to the state of felicity." ¹ To accomplish this, Dante believed that he must present the world in all its complex multiplicity so that men could better understand where they were in relation to everything else, material and spiritual. Misery, according to Dante, is the result of mistaking or distorting one's vision so that only a fragment of reality can be seen, and then taking that fragment for the whole. Felicity becomes possible as the eye learns to see the millions of fragments which make up the universe interacting with one another to create a cosmos.

The view of life presented in the *Comedy* can be called ecological in the largest sense of the term. Dante's Hell is a sink of noxious gasses, polluted water, and denuded forests. The people there have caused their own misery and have created the miserable environment in which they are trapped. They all suffer an impairment of vision which causes them to exaggerate their selfish rights and to satisfy themselves at any cost to others or to the world around them. Purgatory is a place of learning, where men discover what else there is in the world beside themselves. As they increase in understanding and perspective, they begin to see the causes of misery and degradation, and so gradually to become free of them. Paradise is an extremely complicated place, physically and intellectually. The inhabitants see themselves as a part of the complex physical, spiritual, and social life of the world, and they are intensely aware of their own relationships to what they see. Paradise is where human awareness expands to comprehend the complexity of things, rather than reducing complexity to simple principles easily grasped.

Fully as important as the human souls who inhabit Dante's three symbolic environments are the environments themselves. Hell, Purgatory, and Paradise are settings which correspond to the moral and psychological states of the people within them. As each sinner has chosen the particular circumstances which define his life, he has contributed to the creation of an environment which perfectly mirrors his values. In Dante's imaginative vision, human actions build their own most appropriate environment.

HELL

Hell is an image of both moral and biological pollution. Its physical conditions are the environmental equivalent of moral error. The imagery is strikingly similar to that of the modern industrialized, technological, overpopulated, polluted world. Hell is a familiar environment to readers who can feel at home in New York or Los Angeles.

Hell's air is clouded with contaminants and foul odors. The carnal sinners of the second circle whirl in a storm of "black air." [2] Further down, Dante discovers that "the eye could not reach far through the dark air and dense fog." [3] Everyone in Hell squints because of the stinging air and its failure to pass enough light for clear vision. As Dante descends, the air pollution index rises until at the tenth level of Malebolge he is reminded of an ancient disaster at Aegina "where the air was so full of corruption that all the animals, to the little worm, fell dead." [4] Cocytus, the frozen lake at Hell's greatest depth, is clouded by a "thick and murky atmosphere" [5] which all but prevents both breathing and sight.

Hell's waters never run pure. From a spring on the fifth circle the River Styx spurts forth its "water of the blackest purple," [6] which Dante follows downhill past various stagnant bogs notable for their smells and muck. Other rivers run blood or salt tears. All are without nourishment for the barren land through which they pass. Their banks are either lined with stone or, like the channels of Malebolge, "crusted by the exhalation from below with a mould that sticks on them and is repugnant to eyes and nose." [7] When Dante looks deeper, he sees "people plunged in a filth which seemed to have come from human privies." [8] Literal and figurative sewage is the burden of all infernal waters. Styx, Acheron, and Phlegethon drain toward the center of Hell, increasing their burden of tears, blood, sin, and excrement at each descending level. Later, on the Mountain of Purgatory, Dante also learns that the River Lethe which originates in the Garden of Eden collects the cleansed sins of Purgatory before it, too, makes its way to Hell. The sins and excretions of penitent and impenitent alike mingle in the frozen cesspool of Cocytus where Dante's great sewage-laden rivers converge. In Hell, the polluted rivers become instruments of torture for those have polluted them.

Hell's most distinctive characteristic is its hostility to life. Dante's last view of earthly wildlife is an encounter with a leopard, a lion, and a wolf shortly before entering Hell. Though they seem threatening, Dante reacts only in fear of their power and is not repelled by their appearance. The leopard is "light and very swift" and has a "gay skin"; the lion is a dignified animal with its "head high and furious with hunger," and even the she-wolf is not hideous, but appears "in its leanness to be charged with all cravings." [9] The lean agility of these predators is in sharp contrast to the obese and malformed animals which occupy Hell. The few animals in Hell are grotesque mythical beasts with humanoid features such as Cerberus, the three-headed beast who has "red eyes, a beard greasy and black, a great belly, and clawed hands" [10]; the Harpie birds with "wide wings and human necks and faces, feet clawed and their great bellies feathered" [11] or the Monster Geryon who has "the face of a just man" but a serpent's trunk with a scorpion's stinger at its tail. [12] Hell's fauna are grotesque fusions of animal and human forms; genuine animals are not to be found there.

The flora of Hell is similarly maimed. Like its animals, Hell's plants are stunted, deformed, leafless, and lifeless. The third circle is "a plain that rejects every plant from its bed," though it is surrounded by a "doleful wood." [13] Such scenes are frequent in Hell, reminding the reader of the absence of light and water required by plant life. Hell's most memorable plants are perhaps the trees which encase the suicides on the seventh circle: "No green leaves, but of dusky hue; no smooth boughs, but knotted and warped; no fruits there, but poisonous thorns." [14] Like the animals of Hell, these plants are images of distorted humanity. When Dante plucks a twig, words and blood bubble forth together to reveal the vegetative soul of Pier della Vigna, a statesman who had taken his own life when his political fortunes fell. In the view of Irma Brandeis, a professor of literature at Bard College, Pier represents "the suicidal refusal to bend to the reality of change . . . the ultimate deadliness and egocentric cause of all inability to face life when the terms of fortune run counter to desire." [15] This tree is a man who has sought and attained a stunted vegetative existence; many pastoral heroes must share his sterile forest in Hell.[16] Aside from such images, Hell is without greenery or flowers.

All landscapes in Hell are bleak, all natural processes are diseased. Natural elements normally associated with beauty have become ugly reminders of human destructiveness. Though Hell is an alpine setting which taxes Dante's climbing skills, scaling its crags provides no more satisfaction than climbers would find from exploring an open-pit mine. Such anachronistic comparisons are hard to avoid when reading the *Inferno*. Modern oil slicks are suggested by Dante's description of the boiling pitch in which the barrators suffer, especially when Dante compares the sinners to wild ducks, falcons, and hawks and shows them trapped in petroleum: "There was no getting out, they had so beglued their wings." [17] We need not speculate on Dante's mystic premonition of twentieth-century problems; it is enough to recognize that his fourteenth-century attempt to imagine the worst possible human environment describes many of the environmental features which have only now been achieved.

Hell is also overpopulated. Overcrowding is the first misery Dante encounters on his guided tour. Just inside the gate he sees the mob of neutrals, "so long a train of people that I should never have believed death had undone so many." [18] As his journey continues, Dante discovers that everyone in Hell is crowded, spaceless, jammed together with others from whom there is no escape. Trapped togetherness is one of Hell's most characteristic images, repeated on many levels among sinners whose torment is to share a small space with one another: Farinata and Cavalcante in their tiny tomb, Ulysses and Diomed as forked tongues of a single flame, Ugolino and Ruggieri gnawing one another while frozen fast in the ice. High population density is one of Hell's most painful punishments.

As citizens are said always to get the kind of government they deserve, Dante provides his characters with the kind of environment they deserve. The inhabitants of Hell are the people who would make the headlines in any century: political and religious leaders, businessmen and scientists, sex queens, heroes, and freaks. They have in common a single-minded egotism which sets them apart from others and makes their actions seem more significant or dramatic. They are people who have focused their attention upon some fragment of the world, either in an admirable or in a reprehensible way, and made it their own.

Readers are often troubled to find some of their favorite mythical or historical figures in Dante's Hell. Achilles, Dido, Cleopatra, and several famous popes are there, together with others whose names are not well known but whose characters are easily admired: Farinata, the competent and powerful politician who puts the welfare of his party above all else; Francesca, the beautiful woman whose passionate love has made her the victim of murder by a jealous husband; Cavalcante, the dedicated parent who sacrifices himself for his son; Pier della Vigna, the faithful and dedicated civil servant who lost his identity when a bureaucratic shake-up cost him his job. The reader's easy sympathy for such people expresses the recognition that most of us are equally susceptible to such misfortunes, but it also obscures for many readers the essential fact that each sinner has limited his vision of the world to the confines of his personal interests and activities. Each assumes that his private experience of the world is somehow definitive of its basic nature. That is why the sign at the gate says "Abandon hope all ye that enter here." The people in Hell are those who have lost the capacity for seeing themselves in the context of a larger persepctive, and that alone, Dante argues, can relieve their suffering.

The people in Dante's Hell do not know that they are there. Like many moderns, their creation of a joyless environment results from the actions in which they take greatest pride, and they fail to see any causal relationship between those actions and their consequences. As Irma Brandeis puts it, "Knowledge of sin implies repentance as precisely as knowledge of error with respect to some scientific truth implies correction." [19] The sinners do not know that they are in Hell any more than Dante's contemporaries knew that the earth revolves around the sun, for recognition of either fact would necessarily lead to the correction of error. They are prevented from knowing their true state by the pride they take in their uniqueness and specialized talent. Francesca loves being in love, Farinata is proud of his political party, Ugolino lives only to punish his enemy. They feel the pain of their existence, but are at a loss to explain its source. Some, like Francesca and Pier, think they are punished unjustly by a tyrannical God and so solicit pity; others, like Farinata and Satan himself, are proud figures who nobly bear their pain and show only contempt for their surroundings. But "to scorn Hell when one is in it is to scorn the condition of one's soul, the source of one's anguish." [20] Hell is a colossal image of Catch-22: the means for relief from pain are not discernible because the pain is so intense.

Dante's sinners are not punished by God because they have broken the rules of medieval Christian morality. No god and no rules appear in the *Comedy*. Technical sin is of small interest to Dante, who is concerned about the motivations of human actions and their appropriateness to the context in which they occur. Suicide damns Pier because it is an abdication of responsibility, but Cato, also a suicide, has a place of honor in Purgatory because he sacrificed his life in the service of human freedom. Sexuality becomes a prison for Francesca but is the power which Beatrice uses to lure Dante toward Heaven. No action or event in Dante's world has any meaning apart from its context, and it is the context itself, not any external authority, that governs its consequences. The people in Hell are there because they have "lost the good of the intellect." [21] The mind permits humans to understand the world and to act for its welfare and their own. The refusal to understand is its own punishment.

It would have been easy for Dante to represent Hell as a

fearful wilderness setting where nature is symbolic of evil and hostile to man. Much precedent for such an image was ready at hand in medieval tales and legends and in church dogma. Dante's decision to describe Hell as an environment polluted by man and excluding all wild or natural forms is a deliberate innovation which he executes with care and consistency, since it is necessary to his idea that man is the responsible creator of the world he must live in.

PURGATORY

The first line of the *Purgatorio* proclaims that Dante's journey now moves "over better waters." He has also "passed out of the dead air" which had afflicted his eyes and breast,[22] and the sky is now clear from zenith to horizon. Purgatory is an environment congenial to life where trees give shade, dew falls, and grass grows. Air, water, and vegetation are in a healthy state, not cultivated and managed by human gardeners, but self-maintained. What pollution there is comes from man, for as Dante later learns at the top of the mountain, "all the waters that are purest here would seem to have some defilement in them," [23] referring to the memories of human evil bathed away by the River Lethe.

Purgatory is a real mountain. The souls Dante meets there are fellow climbers who share together a common cause, ascent, and who collaborate to achieve it. They work hard together all day and gather in the evening for friendly conversation. Like good climbers everywhere, they "subdue themselves to mount," [24] for they know that the purpose of climbing is to master oneself, not to conquer the mountain.

Purgatory "heals men as they climb" [25] not because it has magical powers but because climbers increase their strength as they ascend by their own efforts.

Hell was shaped like a funnel where vision was directed increasingly inward with each stage of descent; on Purgatory perspectives became broader with each higher level. Dante exploits the relationship between optical and figurative vision to show that Purgatory is a place of learning. The pilgrim's meetings with groups of souls become impromptu seminars on some aspect of nature or experience, moderated generally by professor Virgil, Dante's guide. The curriculum of Purgatory includes whatever can be understood by the intellect.

Virgil is "one that works and reckons and seems always to provide beforehand." [26] He is a competent scholar and a well-informed scientist. In addition to his running commentary which explains the phenomena of Purgatory and includes excursions into such topics as anatomy and physiology, Virgil frequently instructs his pupil in the techniques and limitations of intellectual investigation. His characteristic admonition to Dante is "do not keep thy mind only on one part" [27] as he emphasizes the multiple aspects of knowledge and the subtle relationships among its many parts. His lectures are factual expositions of what is known about man and the world, not speculations into mysteries. His advice is "rest content, race of men, with the *quia*" [28]—with the *that* of facts and experiences—rather than searching for the *why* of final causes.

Short of the mountaintop, Virgil pauses to conduct a graduation ceremony for his pupil. "Over thyself I crown and mitre thee," [29] he tells Dante as he bids him farewell. "I have brought thee here with understanding and with skill. Take henceforth thy pleasure for guide." [30] There is a limit to what professors can help with, and Virgil has reached it. Only when he is fully knowledgeable about the world does Dante become free to let his instincts guide him.

Dante often expresses a belief that instincts govern the behavior of living creatures, including man. The exposition of this doctrine occurs first in one of Virgil's lectures on love, and is later expanded by Beatrice in Paradise. Virgil first equates love with pleasure, explaining that "the mind, created quick to love, is readily moved toward everything that pleases." [31] Dante is troubled to hear that love is a manifestation of innate desires, for that suggests to him that humans are not responsible for their actions and therefore that no free will exists. Virgil cannot solve this problem, but he explains it "as far as reason sees."

> Every substantial form, being both distinct from matter and united with it, holds within itself a specific virtue, which is not perceived except in operation nor is ever demonstrated by its effect, as life in a plant by green leaves. Therefore, whence come the knowledge of primary ideas and the bent to the primary objects of desire, no man knows; they are in you just as in bees zeal to make honey and this primal will admits no deserving of praise or blame. [32]

As plants produce leaves and as bees make honey, so humans behave according to innate desires, the origins of which are unknown. ("Innate" [*innata*] is Dante's word, not an imposition of modern terminology upon Dante's text.) Virgil has more to say about the role of intellect, "the threshold of assent" [33] which has an influence upon innate desires, but leaves the fuller exposition of that matter to

Beatrice, as we will. Virgil merely distinguishes between two types of love, "either natural or of the mind" and specifies that "the natural is always without error, but the other may err through a wrong object or through excess or defect of vigor." [34] The sins punished in Hell and Purgatory are all results of excessive, defective, or misdirected love; that is, of the harmful use of the mind to distort natural behavior. Virgil sounds like a human ethologist in this and in his assertion that the actions of organisms arise from within the organisms themselves and are not the products either of divine will or of environmental determinism.

Souls rise in Purgatory when they succeed in reconciling their minds with their instincts, or in Dante's terms, their will with their desire. No jailers watch over them and no rules of penance are imposed to determine their qualifications for ascent. Statius, a soul just freed from the circle of prodigality, explains to Dante that each soul is "wholly free to change its convent" [35] as soon as its innate desires are consonant with its conscious will concerning the particular sin with which it has been afflicted. All human suffering in Hell and in Purgatory is the consequence of misusing the powers of the mind to limit or distort natural processes which are "always without error."

The final environment of Purgatory is the Earthly Paradise on the mountaintop. Dante finds there no pastoral pleasure garden nor a manicured rural landscape, but a "divine forest green and dense." [36] Thick vegetation creates "the perpetual shade which never lets sun or moon shine there." [37] Something prompted Dante to avoid the standard Christian image of a cultivated and sunny Eden where nature is subordinate to man and to describe instead a complicated landscape which "conceives and brings forth from diverse virtues diverse growths." [38] Diversity is the clearest feature of Dante's Eden, felt in everything from the ground "full of every seed" [39] to the intricate pageantry which displays the entire medieval bestiary of symbolic griffons, foxes, eagles, and dragons along with the complicated forms of church and state on earth and the spiritual transcendence represented by Christ and the heavenly eyes of Beatrice. This Eden is no place of quiet repose, but a busy meeting ground where the processes of nature coalesce with those of society, the human intellect, and the powers of spirit in active interchange. It is here that Beatrice, called by Virgil "a light between truth and the intellect," [40] takes over the guidance of Dante through the even more complicated experiences ahead of him.

PARADISE

Dante's Paradise is not properly an environment at all, but a state of the soul experienced by those who know themselves to be in harmony with the principles and processes of creation. For this reason it is the most difficult part of the poem for many modern readers to relate to. Paradise represents principles and ideas freed from their dependence upon particular entities: love which transcends attachment to things, process without active agents, relationships without objects, plurality without singularity, truth without facts, and pure light perceived directly rather than reflected from surfaces. "Beyond our wont I fixed my eyes upon the sun," [41] Dante announces at the beginning; Paradise is where he learns to look directly at the sources of life, not by wearing protective glasses or studying reflected images, but by perfecting his eyesight.

Virgil conducted Dante as far as good scientific analysis can conduct human beings, to the point of factual understanding of the structure and meaning of the world. The vision of integration which Dante finds in Paradise is suprascientific, though inclusive of the science of Dante's period and consistent with it. It is also suprahuman in the sense that it passes beyond the levels of human experience which language is suited to describe. Dante reminds his readers that "the passing beyond humanity [*transumanar*] cannot be set in words," [42] because words, however figurative or abstract, depend upon their relationship to things and events. Virgil, the inquiring and comprehending mind, is thus no longer enough to serve Dante's needs, and he is superseded by an image which combines rational knowledge with spiritual insight and wordless wonder, the beautiful woman Beatrice.

The role played by the historical Beatrice in Dante's life and her symbolic role in the *Comedy* are subtle and complex. In the *Paradiso* Dante uses her to represent a fulfilled human being who has realized intellectually and spiritually her true relationship to reality and who thus radiates beauty united with intelligence. She has everything that Virgil had, plus the powers of emotional and esthetic attraction which make her loved as well as respected.

Like a good scientist, Beatrice believes that "all things whatsoever have order among themselves." [43] Her concept of order, however, is a rich synthesis of material and spiritual reality which has nothing mechanistic about it. Beatrice is a vitalist who believes that there is an "instinct" (*instinto*) in all things which "binds the earth together and makes it one." [44] Her doctrine is derived from scholastic theology, which defines God's love as a kind of divine mucilage holding the world together and governing all change and growth. Unlike some church dogmatists, Beatrice emphasizes that the instinct for order is *internal* to the creatures of the universe, not regulated by a divine intelligence, and that it operates the same in all forms of life: "Not only the creatures that are without intelligence does this bow shoot, but those also that have intellect and love." [45] The metaphor which likens instinct to a bow and creatures to arrows reaffirms the belief expressed throughout the *Comedy* that the power of life is internal to living creatures, and that man alone has the ability to misdirect that power through errors of the intellect. As the souls in Hell aimed toward selfish aggrandizement and those in Purgatory learned of higher targets, so the souls in Paradise have achieved the unity of the bow of instinct (desire) and the arrow of intellect (will) centered on the target of universal order.

Throughout the *Paradiso*, great emphasis is placed upon diversity as a necessary condition for stability and order. When Beatrice instructs Dante in the complicated organization of Paradise, she reminds him that "diverse virtue makes diverse alloy" [46] and that he should not expect to find here the relative simplicity of Hell and Purgatory. The soul of Charles Martel later extends this principle to include behavioral as well as structural diversity, arguing that humans must "live in diverse ways for diverse tasks" [47] as other natural creatures do. He concludes his explanation of diversity with an admonition: "If the world below gave its mind to the foundation that nature lays and followed it, it would be well for its people." [48] Though his argument is often interpreted as an instance of the medieval effort to hold people in the social status of their birth, it is evident from the context that Dante intends also to establish diversity of human and natural elements as a necessary condition of stability.

Dante's *Paradiso* is not an abstract conception which rejects the validity of physical or sensual experience. Such criticism applies to much medieval literature, but to Dante not at all. His Paradise is a place where bodily experience is perfected, not rejected. However spiritual or symbolic Beatrice may be, Dante never lets the reader forget that she is also a beautiful woman whose appearance thrills him as often as do her words. And when Beatrice explains the resurrection of the body, she is happy to assure Dante that on Judgment Day, "the organs of the body shall be strong for all that can delight us." [49] Paradise is no ascetic retreat, but a completed experience in which sensuality is appreciated for its meaning and context and therefore enjoyed more fully than when it is pursued only for personal gratification.

Dante never rejects the world even when he perceives its smallness from the threshold of the Empyrean. His astronaut's views of earth, like the one we have acquired technologically in our time, reminds him that the earth is a small element of a larger system, a dependent part rather than an end in itself. "I saw this globe such that I smiled at its paltry semblance," [50] says Dante. There is no scorn in this view, but rather compassion for the earth's inhabitants on their "little threshing-floor." [51] Dante's entry into Paradise is not an escape from the earth but the acquisition of a larger perspective from which to understand it.

Even Dante's final beatific vision is an image of the integration of the world's parts, one of which is mankind. There is no ordering deity in human form controlling the universe from the upper reaches of Paradise, but only pure light, dazzling in its clarity and intensity. Dante's visual schooling as he has passed through the realms of being has prepared him to gaze at the source of light directly, and even to make out some images within it:

> I dared to fix my look on the Eternal Light
> so long that I spent all my sight upon it!
> In its depth I saw that it contained, bound
> by love in one volume, that which is scattered
> in leaves through the universe, substances
> and accidents and their relations as it
> were fused together in such a way that what
> I tell of is a simple light. I think I
> saw the universal form of this complex,
> because in telling of it I feel my joy expand.[52]

The universal form is a complex of relationships, inclusive of all life, thought, and spirit. As Dante stares, his vision improves further and he begins to see circles and colors and movements which appear to be "painted with our like-ness."[53] The image of mankind, in some obscure way, is a part of the image of universal form, and Dante strains in an effort "to see how the image was fitted to the circle and how it has its place there, but my own wings were not sufficient for that."[54] Mankind is somehow amidst the substances, accidents, and relationships of universal order, but Dante's vision and his poem end with the unanswerable question of how, precisely, man fits in.

Dante's Paradise, and especially the beatific vision at its height, is a climax ecosystem in the ultimate sense of the term. Ecologists have lately objected to the use of the term *climax* because it suggests finality and completeness, which are foreign to natural processes, and tends to encourage people to think of nature in static terms. But the climax of a literary work is the moment when all themes, moods, and ideas unite in a flash of insight and their genuine relationships suddenly become clear. It is not a sustainable insight, but is followed inevitably by a denouement, which returns the reader once more to the more prosaic world of fragmentary events and their uncertain consequences. Literary, metaphysical, sexual, and ecological climaxes are not permanently frozen states of being, but momentary epiphanies from which less intense and less perfect events must follow. Dante must return from his high vision to a desk somewhere in tortured Italy so that he can write a poem telling of what he has seen.

DANTE'S MODERN COMEDY

The twentieth-century French philosopher Jacques Maritain spoke of Dante's "innocence" and of his "luck." [55] Dante was innocent in the sense that he unashamedly assumed that his private experience was symbolic of the life of all mankind. His love of Beatrice stood for all love, his life in politics illustrated the meaning of politics, and his vision of universal order was treated as a revelation of genuine cosmic integration. Dante's poem is unique in its fusion of the intensely personal with the highest levels of abstraction, and in its convincing demonstration that the two are compatible.

Dante was "lucky" because his life coincided with a climactic moment in medieval Christianity just prior to its disintegration. Dante's time made available what Maritain calls "existential certainties" which affirmed that the intricate complexities of the world are intelligible, that human thought and action are somehow a part of that complexity, and that all life is integrated according to principles which man must recognize and adapt to if he hopes to attain fulfillment. Dante's world permitted these basic assumptions as no period since has been able to do, and permitted Dante to construct in his poem the last image of an integrated universe before the fragmentations of the modern world emerged.

From a modern, scientific perspective, Dante's medieval world appears to be drastically misinformed about the nature of things. Dante lived in a world that still did not know about nuclear warfare, about the profound changes that technology was to make upon human perceptions, about indeterminacy in physics and neurosis in the subconscious, about space travel and the evolution of man from animal origins. Nevertheless, modern readers discover that Dante describes accurately the specific characteristics of their own felt experience. The nature of human pain and joy has not changed in the half-dozen centuries since Dante, but the world has come to resemble Hell more than ever before.

Medieval Christianity provided humanity with a way to think about the world and to respond to its conditions as participants in an order larger than themselves. However complicated, the world appeared to have a meaningful structure, and a human being's welfare appeared to depend upon his understanding of that structure and his ability to coordinate his own life with it. During the succeeding centuries, Western civilization has operated largely on the assumption that the world must be shaped and managed to conform to human needs and interests. The consequences of that assumption are evident in the disruption of the natural environment and in the disorder of the modern soul.

Dante explained the title of his poem by referring to the classic definition of comic form as the passage from pain to pleasure: "At the beginning it is horrible and fetid, for it is hell; and in the end it is prosperous, desirable, and gracious, for it is Paradise." It is also comic in that its language is "lax and humble," as opposed to the elevated and dignified discourse of tragic poetry.[56] Erich Auerbach, the late German scholar of comparative literature, added that Dante's complicated mixture of literary styles has the effect of lifting the comic mode of expression to a new level of sublimity never before attained.[57] But the poem is also comic in the sense used throughout this book: it is an image of human adaptation to the world and acceptance of its given conditions without escape, rebellion, or egotistic insistence upon human centrality. Dante's *Comedy* is cosmic, not divine.

Mann's Felix Krull and Dante's pilgrim have in common their belief that life is an art form. Irma Brandeis says that Dante's "love of God does not . . . result in a turning away from the world, but on the contrary a new and indestructible turning towards it in an emotion that bears comparison to nothing so much as to the feelings generated by a perfect work of art." [58] This is not the tragic-pastoral vision of a world of raw materials destined to receive artistic form through skillful manipulation by man, but the comic-picaresque image of a beautiful world which human creativeness must complement. Felix Krull's dictum, "He who truly loves the world must shape himself to please it," describes accurately the meaning of Dante's philosophy and the strategy of his art.

Ecologists and environmentalists trudge sadly through our twentieth-century hells and purgatories like Virgil, analyzing the causes and effects of corruption and instructing us about available remedies. They describe well enough the meaning of sin, but not how to love. Beauty and spiritual insight, the province of Beatrice, are too easily relegated to the realm of the humanities. Humanists, on the other hand, can easily forget that beauty has a body as intricate as its soul. A little joint instruction from Virgil and Beatrice in the comedy of survival would be a wholesome experience for the many Dantes now awakening to find themselves lost in a dark wood.

NINE

The Sky
Within the Earth

THE GERMAN NOVELIST ROBERT MUSIL CHARACTERIZED THE development of Western science since the Renaissance in his 1930 novel, *The Man Without Qualities*. "It was in the sixteenth century," Musil says, "that people gradually ceased trying, as they had been all through two thousand years of religious and philosophic speculation, to penetrate into the secrets of Nature, and instead contented themselves, in a way that can only be called superficial, with investigations of its surface." [1] Science merely sat down on the earth, "making contact with a dependable and not really dignified part of the body." With his buttocks on the ground and his eyes straight ahead, the post-Renaissance scientist has measured the surfaces of the earth, and the earth, Musil continues, "has shown itself uncommonly susceptible, and since that contact took place has let inventions, conveniences and discoveries be wormed out of it in downright miraculous quantities." [2] It might be added that twentieth-century environmental crisis is also a consequence of manipulating the surface of things oblivious to deeper contexts.

Dante's religious and philosophic concept of nature does not belong in a twentieth-century world. The modern bottom is comfortable sitting on the earth and feeling its warmth, however superficial that contact may be. It is easy to admire Dante's integrated perspective and to regret that a *Comedy* such as his can no longer be written. Medieval Christendom provided Dante with a model universe comprehensive enough to include all known orders of life and experience. Dante knew well that it was a model, a stage setting upon which he could put to work the expressive illusions of his poetic art. So convincing was the illusion that modern readers can easily mistake Dante's poem for an official road map of medieval cosmology. The poem is in fact just what Dante said it was: a comedy intended to illustrate the conditions of misery and felicity, with suggestions about what must be done to qualify for one or the other. Although the model no longer fits with modern scientific ideas of the world, the prerequisites for misery and felicity have remained essentially unchanged.

Since the time of Dante, more and more energy has been devoted to parsing the world into small and manageable chunks suitable to the purposes of the modern mentality. The sense of fragmentation which has accompanied an earthbound scientific culture is an increasing source of misery for many, and its few felicities are transient and unsatisfying. Particularly painful is the awareness that the natural world and its processes have themselves suffered disintegration, in the literal sense of the term. If the integrity of the earth disappears, no other kind of integrity can have any meaning. Some such awareness lies at the root of contemporary hope and enthusiasm over ecology. From a science with its bottom on the earth has come a model which promises to reconnect the sundered fragments and to find within nature keys to wholeness like those which Dante attributed to his heavenly model. Animals now seem more likely to enlighten us than angels, and nature more than God.

Still, ecology is as much a humanly created model as medieval cosmology was. It is a system available for correlating human experiences, including but not limited to scientific experiences and observations of nature. The significance of the ecological model will be determined by the breadth and depth of what is to be included within it. If it integrates only those measurements of the surface which for Musil characterized post-Renaissance science, then it will become just one more interdisciplinary device, useful but spiritually powerless. More hopeful is the prospect that ecology will also offer connective links of large scope, including the art and thought of human culture as these are consistent with a healthy natural environment. An ecological model of the world will incorporate principles of integration resembling those derived by Dante from his theological model, including a holistic conception of the world's structure, an artistic view of mankind's role on earth, and a capacity to think and to live in the comic mode.

A Whole Earth

Intellectual specialization, invented in the Renaissance and developed as a way of life since then, has been challenged seriously during recent decades. Movements intended to bridge the separations among specialized cate-

gories of knowledge and thought have popped up everywhere in the twentieth century. Such movements have
influenced the sciences, education, religion, politics, the
arts, and literature. The intellectual vocabulary now includes such terms as biochemistry, geopolitics, physical
chemistry, bioethics, comparative religion, and comparative
literature. The Greek word *eikos* ("habitation") has supplied names for ecology as an interdisciplinary science, and
for ecumenical movements which seek unity among Christian churches. Political and economic counterparts are to
be found in the United Nations, the Common Market, and
in many lesser structures of cooperation and detente. Rudi-
mentary and fragile as such coalitions may be, they suggest
that we may be near the beginning of a new period of con-
nectedness in Western history. These experimental movements will not lead automatically to high spiritual visions
like Dante's, but they are small steps in that direction.

Specialization of knowledge, mankind's initial response
to the Renaissance discovery of human freedom, must be
counterbalanced by a concept of unity. Shifting the focus
from God to man leaves man free to achieve the large
perspective upon the world formerly attributed to God
alone. Whatever else he may have been, God was surely
interdisciplinary. Mankind's inheritance from the death of
God might have been the gift of an expanded world vision
rather than the assumption of human pride and power
which has been characteristic of post-Renaissance humanism and science.

The Last Whole Earth Catalog contains this unidentified
quotation: "We can't put it all together; it *is* all together."
It is not up to mankind to create a new world ecology, but
to appreciate the ecological structures which have evolved

over millions of years without human guidance. Four centuries of specialization have not severed the essential interconnections of the world, but they have weakened the human capacity to understand them. The unitive movements of recent years are attempts to reintroduce process and relationship as principles of knowledge and action to replace the unhealthy influences of specialization and disjunctive abstraction.

One Renaissance thinker who interpreted mankind's new estate as an opportunity for broader understanding rather than for increased self-admiration was the sixteenth-century French essayist, Michel de Montaigne. Near the end of his life, Montaigne reached the conclusion that "our great and glorious masterpiece is to live appropriately." [3] Mankind's special talent, in other words, is to understand where humanity belongs in relation to the rest of creation, and that is a high talent compatible with a thoroughly admirable conception of humanity. It is no insult to the dignity of mankind to say that our highest function may be to discover our appropriate role in a world that does not seem to have been designed to serve exclusively human purposes.

Appropriate living is life in its total context, which now includes evolutionary as well as cultural history, plus the multiple contemporary forms of life which need a whole earth as much as humans do. Spiritual and artistic creativity are not special powers provided so that humans can transcend the natural world, but features of human biological development useful for connecting humanity more deeply with the world. The behavior of animals, the interrelated processes of ecological nature, the multimillion-year past shared by the surviving components of the earth, and the human spirit all require synthesis, not separation.

Earth Art

As ecological understanding brings about changes in man's relationship with his environment, art forms will inevitably undergo similar changes. The pastoral image of a domestic and tamed landscape swept clean of dangers and discomforts, inviting though it may seem, in fact represents ecological disruption which is harmful to nature and ultimately to people. The pastoral mode, whether it is expressed in literature, in agriculture, in politics, or in nature-loving social movements, leads necessarily toward ecological damage and toward human dissatisfaction.

Human beings, who have long regarded the earth as raw material to be shaped to human needs, are at last beginning to regard themselves as raw materials needing to be shaped toward greater compatibility with the earth. Mankind is derived from the natural world, not the other way around. Both Dante's pilgrim and Thomas Mann's Felix Krull share that assumption and build their careers upon it. Both use their intellect and imagination as means to modify and perfect themselves toward maximum agreement with the world as they find it. Their self-discipline is an artistic technique using uniquely human powers for purposes of adaptation to a given reality. The principles governing this picaresque process are derived from attentiveness to the world and its creatures, and from an accurate appraisal of the self and its potentials.

Picaresque immorality and Dante's heresies are merely

infractions against arbitrary social codes of their respective cultures. Neither the inviolability of personal property which Krull ignores, nor the infallibility of the Roman pope which Dante rejects, are principles of nature, nor are they necessary human laws. Great art goes beyond the cultural biases of particular times and places to represent forms of deeper origin. Relatively few such esthetic patterns seem to serve for all humanity, and these persist regardless of great variations of language, geography, and intellectual or social context.

Humanism has been consistently anthropocentric in its assumptions concerning art. Since art is created only by humans, it has seemed reasonable to suppose that its significance is limited to human history and to the functions of language and symbol which uniquely characterize the human mind. But the origins of art more likely lie in the prehuman evolutionary past of mankind. Before human consciousness or civilization appeared, the primate ancestors of mankind had developed the emotional and behavioral patterns which were later to become the specific ethology of *homo sapiens.* Like other animals, prehuman primates evolved an inner life appropriate to their anatomy and physiology and to the ecology of their environments. It is to this profound level of experience that the greatest art returns us, and from this level that it draws its most expressive images of human experience.

Art recalls mankind to experiences which are older than mankind itself, experiences that are shared by man's evolutionary forebears and probably by many other animals as well. The recurrent patterns in art and literature are images of life, not merely of human life. Cultural contexts provide the languages and symbols, and they dictate the external forms of expression, but the essential patterns of human esthetic experience are innate, derived from our prehuman ancestors. They do not separate us from nature but unite us with it.

The Comedy of Fulfillment

Simple survival is not enough to satisfy the needs of any species. It is not enough for individuals to live their allotted spans and reproduce new generations; the species itself must undergo change in response to environmental and genetic variations, although individuals must live within the limits of their particular endowments received at birth. All creatures must fulfill whatever is potentially within them in accordance with the environment that is actually around them.

The comic mode of behavior seems to be the most appropriate expression of animal and human gifts. It is respectful of the prerequisites for life and is careful in its maintenance of them. When ecological balances are disturbed, comic action seeks their restoration. What is more, comedy seeks joy. For those animals whose behavior is mainly governed by instinct, fulfillment is a relatively easy matter. Among human animals it becomes more complicated, for the human will is capable of contradicting instinctual desires. Human comedy seeks reconciliation of will and desire rather than the conquest of one by the other. The successful accomplishment of that comic integration is what Dante calls felicity.

Human comedy does not offer a proud view of mankind but an accurate one, mindful of human limitations and modest in its assessment of human potentials. With little guilt over the past and little expectation from the future, the comic mode seeks its fulfillment from the present. Its greatest pleasures arise from the satisfaction of basic bodily needs and from the flexibility of the human mind as it responds to the ironies and bewilderments of daily experience. Yet the comic perspective is not frivolous. Its themes are birth, life, conflict, reproduction, necessity, death, and the fulfillment of human needs. Its message is that these are essential features of existence which must be accommodated and, if possible, understood. Even if they cannot be understood, they must be accepted and borne with good grace. Although comedy fails to curse the world or to make gigantic demands of it, it is not shallow. The humor of comedy is most often an attempt to deflate the overinflated, not to trivialize what is genuinely important. Comedy is serious about life even in its lightest moments.

Scientific ecology and literary comedy are consistent with a rich and diverse human culture. Mankind cannot afford the consequences of human self-aggrandizement, but fulfillment may lie in a knowing and spirited immersion in the processes of nature, illuminated by the adaptive and imaginative human mind. In literature or in ecology, comedy enlightens and enriches human experience without trying to transform either mankind or the world.

Reference Notes
Suggested Readings
Index

Reference Notes

CHAPTER TWO:

The Comic Mode

1. David Grene and Richmond Lattimore, *The Complete Greek Tragedies* (Chicago: University of Chicago Press, 1959), 2:26.

2. John Barth, *Giles Goat-Boy* (New York: Fawcett, 1967), 323.

3. Susanne Langer, *Feeling and Form* (New York: Charles Scribner's Sons, 1953), 345.

4. Konrad Lorenz, *On Aggression* (New York: Bantam Books, 1967), 171–173, 284–287.

5. Charles F. Hockett and Robert Ascher, "The Human Revolution," *Current Anthropology* 5, No. 3 (1964), 140.

6. Joseph Heller, *Catch-22* (New York: Dell, 1961), 251–252.

CHAPTER THREE:

Literary Tragedy and Ecological Catastrophe

1. Sophocles, *Antigone,* in David Grene and Richmond Lattimore, *The Complete Greek Tragedies* (Chicago: University of Chicago Press, 1959), 2:170–171.

2. Exodus 32.

3. Cedric Whitman, *Homer and the Heroic Tradition* (New York: Norton, 1958), 199.

4. Ibid., 220.

5. Joseph Wood Krutch, *The Modern Temper* (New York: Harcourt, Brace & World, 1956), 92.

6. Ibsen, *The Master Builder,* in Evert Sprinchorn, ed., *The Genius of the Scandinavian Theater* (New York: Mentor, 1956), 238.

7. Alain Robbe-Grillet, *For a New Novel*, trans. Richard Howard (New York: Grove Press, 1965), 57.

8. Ibid., 72–73.

CHAPTER FOUR:

Hamlet and the Animals

1. Harold Clarke Goddard, *The Meaning of Shakespeare* (Chicago: University of Chicago Press, 1951), 2:357.

2. Konrad Lorenz, *Studies in Animal and Human Behavior* (Cambridge: Harvard University Press, 1971), 2:149.

3. Ireneas Eibl-Eibesfeldt, *Ethology* (New York: Holt, 1970), 314.

4. *Ibid.*, 315. See also Konrad Lorenz, "Die angeborenen Formen möglicher Erfahrung," *Zeitschrift für Tierpsychologie,* 5 (1943), 235–409.

5. Goddard, *Meaning of Shakespeare,* 1:364.

6. See R. M. Schenkel, "Zum Problem der Territorialität und des Markierens bei Säugern—am Beispiel des Schwarzen Nashorns und des Löwen," *Zeitschrift für Tierpsychologie,* 23 (1966), 593–626.

7. Erik Erikson, "The Ontogeny of Ritualization in Man," *Philosophical Transactions of the Royal Society,* 772 (1966), 251B, 337–349.

8. Konrad Lorenz, "Knowledge, Belief, and Freedom," in Paul Weiss, *Hierarchically Organized Systems* (New York: Hafner, 1971), 248.

9. Homer, *Iliad,* trans. Richard Lattimore (Chicago: University of Chicago Press, 1951), bk. 22, pp. 261–267.

10. J. W. v. Goethe, *Wilhelm Meister's Apprenticeship* (1796), trans. Thomas Carlyle (London, 1851), bk. 4, chap. 13.

11. Konrad Lorenz, personal conversation, tape recording in author's possession.

CHAPTER FIVE:

The Pastoral and the Picaresque

1. Virgil, *Works of Virgil,* trans. J. W. MacKail (New York: Random House, 1950), 267.

2. Ibid., 266.

3. *Satires of Juvenal,* trans. Rolfe Humphries (Bloomington: Indiana University Press, 1958), 42.

4. Boccaccio, *Decameron,* trans. Richard Aldington (New York: Dell, 1962), 32, 35.

5. Ibid., 173.

6. Ibid., 174.

7. Ebenezer Howard, *Garden Cities of Tomorrow* (Cambridge: MIT Press, 1965), 44.

8. Leo Marx, *The Machine in the Garden* (New York: Oxford University Press, 1964), 141.

9. Thomas Jefferson, *Notes on the State of Virginia,* Query 19, quoted in Marx, *Machine,* 124.

10. Jefferson to William Short, November 28, 1814, quoted in Marx, *Machine,* 144.

11. Howard, *Garden Cities,* 48.

12. Ibid.

13. Marx, *Machine,* 364.

14. *The Pleasaunte Historie of Lazarillo de Tormes,* trans. David Rowland (London, 1586); ed. J. E. V. Crofts (Oxford: B. Blackwell, 1924), 11.

15. William Faulkner, *The Reivers* (New York: Random House, 1962), 121.

16. Johann von Grimmelshausen, *Simplicius Simplicissimus,* trans. George Schulz-Behrend (Indianapolis: Bobbs-Merrill, 1965), 27.

17. Ibid., 80.

18. Ibid., 84.

19. Ibid., 153.

20. Ibid., 215.

21. Ibid., 264.

22. Joseph Heller, *Catch-22* (New York: Dell, 1955), 21.

23. Ibid., 30.

24. Ibid., 24.

25. Ibid., 312.

26. Ibid., 461.

27. Ibid., 463.

28. Thomas Mann, *Confessions of Felix Krull, Confidence Man,* trans. Denver Lindley (New York: Alfred Knopf, 1955), 13.

29. Ibid., 65.

30. Ibid., 11.

31. Ibid., 90.

32. Ibid., 149.
33. Ibid., 22.
34. Ibid., 106.
35. Ibid., 298.
36. Ibid., 301.
37. Ibid., 304.
38. Ibid.
39. Ibid., 271.
40. Ibid., 317.
41. Niccolò Machiavelli, *The Prince,* trans. Luigi Ricci, rev. E. R. P. Vincent (New York: Mentor, 1952), 84.
42. Ibid.
43. Ibid., 93.
44. Ibid., 92.
45. Ibid., 112.
46. Ibid., 122–123.
47. Ibid., 119.
48. Heller, *Catch-22,* 456.

CHAPTER SIX:

Ecological Esthetics

1. A general discussion of domestication effects is to be found in Konrad Lorenz, *Studies in Animal and Human Behavior* (London: Methuen, 1971), 2:167–172; 231–238. My discussion of domestication draws upon this source and upon my notes from personal discussions with Dr. Lorenz in November, 1971.

2. Lorenz, *Studies,* 2:167.

3. Paul Weiss, "Beauty and the Beast: Life and the Rule of Order," *Scientific Monthly,* 81:6 (1955), 288.

4. Ibid., 296.

5. Ibid., 297.

6. Susanne Langer, *Feeling and Form* (New York: Charles Scribner's Sons, 1953).

7. Ibid., 82.

CHAPTER SEVEN:

Ingredients for an Environmental Ethic

1. William Faulkner, *The Reivers* (New York: Random House, 1962), 122.

2. Paul Shepard, *The Tender Carnivore and the Sacred Game* (New York: Charles Scribner's Sons, 1973).

3. Jean-Paul Sartre, "Existentialism is a Humanism," in Walter Arnold Kaufmann, *Existentialism from Dostoyevsky to Sartre* (New York: Meridian, 1956), 297–298.

4. E. M. Forster, *Two Cheers for Democracy* (New York: Harcourt, Brace & World, 1938), 68.

5. Fyodor Dostoyevsky, *The Brothers Karamazov*, trans. David Magarshack (New York: Penguin Books, 1958), 287–288.

6. Fyodor Dostoyevsky, *The Devils*, trans. David Magarshack (Baltimore: Penguin Books, 1953), 612.

7. Dostoyevsky, *The Brothers Karamazov*, 77.

8. Stuart Hampshire, "Morality and Pessimism," *New York Review of Books*, January 25, 1973, 33–34.

9. Faulkner, *The Reivers*, 121. (Italics mine.)

10. Thomas Mann, *Confessions of Felix Krull, Confidence Man*, trans. Denver Lindley (New York: Knopf, 1955), 65.

CHAPTER EIGHT

The Comedy of Dante's *Comedy*

1. Dante, Epistola 10, *Letter to Can Grande della Scala*, trans. P. H. Wickstead, in James H. Smith and Edd W. Parks, *The Great Critics* (New York: W. W. Norton, 1951), 148.

2. Dante Alighieri, *The Divine Comedy*, trans. John D. Sinclair (London: The Bodley Head, 1948), *Inferno*, 5. 50. Quotations used are from this parallel prose translation; numbers refer to canto and lines in the Italian text.

3. Ibid., 9. 5–6.

4. Ibid., 29. 60–62.

5. Ibid., 21. 38.

6. Ibid., 7. 104.

7. Ibid., 18. 106–108.

8. Ibid., 114–115.

9. Ibid., 1. 31–50.

10. Ibid., 6. 16–19.

11. Ibid., 12. 13–16.

12. Ibid., 17. 10–13.

13. Ibid., 14. 10–11.

14. Ibid., 13. 4–7.

15. Irma Brandeis, *The Ladder of Vision* (New York: Anchor Books, 1962), 62.

16. See chapter 5, The Pastoral and the Picaresque, for discussion of pastoral values, plants, and suicide.

17. *Inferno,* 22. 142–143.

18. Ibid., 3. 55–57.

19. Brandeis, *Ladder,* 29.

20. Ibid., 49.

21. *Inferno,* 3. 18.

22. *Purgatorio,* 1. 18–19.

23. Ibid., 28. 24–30.

24. Ibid., 13. 103.

25. Ibid., line 3.

26. *Inferno,* 24. 25.

27. *Purgatorio,* 10. 46.

28. Ibid., 3. 38.

29. Ibid., 27. 142.

30. Ibid., 130–133.

31. Ibid., 18. 19–20.

32. Ibid., 46–60.

33. Ibid., 18. 63.

34. Ibid., 17. 92–96.

35. Ibid., 21. 62.

36. Ibid., 28. 2.

37. Ibid., 32–33.

38. Ibid., 113–114.

39. Ibid., 119.

40. Ibid., 6. 45.

41. *Paradiso,* 1. 54.

42. Ibid., 70.

43. Ibid., 103–104.

44. Ibid., 114–117.

45. Ibid., 118–120.

46. Ibid., 2. 139.

47. Ibid., 8. 119.

48. Ibid., 143–145.

49. Ibid., 14. 59–60.

50. Ibid., 22. 135.

51. Ibid., 151.

52. Ibid., 33. 82–93.

53. Ibid., 131.

54. Ibid., 137–139.

55. Jacques Maritain, *Creative Intuition in Art and Poetry* (New York: Meridian, 1955), 264–281.

56. Dante, *Epistola* 10, p. 147.

57. Eric Auerbach, *Mimesis: The Representation of Reality in Western Literature* (New York: Doubleday, 1957), 159–165.

58. Brandeis, *Ladder,* 104.

CHAPTER NINE

The Sky Within the Earth

1. Robert Musil, *The Man Without Qualities,* trans. Eithne Wilkins and Ernst Kaiser (New York: Capricorn Books, 1965), 359.

2. Musil, *The Man Without Qualities,* 360.

3. Michel de Montaigne, *The Complete Essays of Montaigne,* trans. Donald M. Frame (Stanford: Stanford University Press, 1948), 851.

Suggested Readings

LITERATURE FOR ECOLOGICAL STUDY

The literary works discussed in the text are but a few of the many suitable for ecological study. Those in the following list would reward further study. Annotations suggest possible topics in literary ecology appropriate to each.

Barth, John. *The Sot-Weed Factor.* New York: Doubleday & Co., 1960.

A comic-picaresque account of the early settlement of America in which the heroic rhetoric of Western culture is displayed against the background of American wilderness, revealing its inadequacy to the new land.

Borges, Jorge Luis. *The Book of Imaginary Beings* (1967). Trans. the author and N. T. di Giovanni. New York: Avon Books, 1969.

A collection of literary and mythical animals interpreted by a major contemporary author. Illustrative of the psychological and cultural depth of animal imagery in literature.

Cervantes, Miguel de. *Don Quixote de la Mancha* (1605). Trans. Samuel Putnam. New York: Viking Press, 1951.

The world's greatest work of mock-heroic comedy, important to the modern development of picaresque literature. All essential issues of literary ecology are included.

Faulkner, William. *Go Down Moses* (1942). New York: Modern Library, 1955.

The destruction of the wilderness of the American South, with its consequences for Indian, black, and white people and for the human soul. The extended section, "The Bear," concentrates on the conflict between human exploitation and wilderness preservation.

Gilgamesh (ca. third millennium B.C.). English version by N. K. Sandars. Baltimore: Penguin Books, 1960.

An ancient Mesopotamian culture hero's attempt to reconcile the needs of civilization with biological necessities (sex, death, sleep). Rich imagery of wilderness and wildlife, including an episode of animal-human interchangeability.

Goethe, Johann Wolfgang von. *Faust, a Tragedy in Two Parts* (1808 and 1832). Trans. Charles E. Passage. Indianapolis: Bobbs-Merrill, 1965.

A comprehensive image of the relationships between humanity and nature by the modern world's best-known poet-scientist. Faust symbolizes the tragic tradition of Western civilization and its ideology of nature.

Hasek, Jaroslav. *The Good Soldier: Schweik* (1922). Trans. Paul Selver. New York: Signet Classics, 1963.

A picaresque antiwar novel of World War I in which noble idealism is weighed against comic survival and is found wanting.

Homer. *Iliad* (ca. eighth century B.C.). Trans. Richmond Lattimore. Chicago: University of Chicago Press, 1951.

One of the world's most comprehensive accounts of aggression and its role in human emotions and culture. Powerful imagery of animals and nature throughout.

Kazantzakis, Nikos. *The Odyssey: A Modern Sequel* (1938). Trans. Kimon Friar. New York: Simon & Schuster, 1958.

An attempt to reconcile modern vitalism with ancient patterns of quest literature. Spiritual evolution is dramatized in relation to biological evolution.

Lagerlöf, Selma. *The Story of Gösta Berling* (1891). Trans. Robert Bly. New York: Signet Classics, 1962.

A Scandinavian picaresque novel, strong in its representation of Northern European wilderness and its effects upon human psychology and social relationships.

Mann, Thomas. *Joseph and His Brothers* (1934–1944). Trans. Helen T. Lowe-Porter. New York: Alfred A. Knopf, 1956.

A narrative of the mythic origins of Hebraic cultural traditions, in which picaresque values play a major role.

——. *A Man and His Dog* (1918). Trans. Helen T. Lowe-Porter; and included in Mann's *Stories of Three Decades*. New York: Alfred A. Knopf, 1936.

A reflection upon relationships between humans and animals revealed through speculations about the differences between an artist and his animal friend.

Melville, Herman. *Moby Dick* (1851). Boston: Houghton Mifflin (Riverside Editions), 1956.

The spirit of man in battle with an animal and the sea. A powerful novel in the tragic mode showing the capacity of the tragic spirit for elevating mankind while destroying both man and nature.

Montaigne, Michel de. *The Complete Essays of Montaigne* (1572–1588). Trans. Donald M. Frame. Stanford: Stanford University Press, 1948.

Mature reflections upon the relations between man and nature in the light of new ideas emerging from Renaissance thought. Montaigne illustrates a crucial stage in Western cultural concepts of nature and spirit.

Musil, Robert. *The Man Without Qualities* (1930). Trans. Eithne Wilkins and Ernst Kaiser. New York: Capricorn Books, 1965.

A novel of modern man deprived of his customary characteristics by a technological society. A fictional inventory of the natural qualities remaining to mankind when human culture fails.

Njal's Saga (ca. 1280). Trans. Magnus Magnusson. Baltimore: Penguin Books, 1960.

A narrative of the transplantation of a culture from Scandinavia to the harsher environment of Iceland, particularly revealing for its descriptions of consequent changes in beliefs and social institutions, and for its images of human aggression combined with comedy.

Song of the Nibelungs, The (ca. 1200). Trans. Frank G. Ryder. Detroit: Wayne State University Press, 1962.

Heroic revenge in the tragic mode, and its disastrous consequences for a civilization. Medieval European attitudes toward nature parallel human relationships, all of which lead toward destruction.

Thoreau, Henry David. *Walden* (1854). New York: Modern Library, 1950.

The prototype and source of many recent American attitudes toward nature, compounded of traditional pastoralism and semiscientific personal reflections.

Tolstoy, Leo. *Anna Karenina* (1877). Trans. David Magarshack. New York: Signet Classics, 1961.

Themes of urban civilization are contrasted with those of rural agriculture, which Tolstoy identifies with nature. Male and female sexuality is explored in depth.

————. *War and Peace* (1869). Trans. Louise and Aylmer Maude. New York: W. W. Norton & Co., 1966.

The cultural and psychological conditions of aggression are presented by Tolstoy as they relate to his concept of nature. The Norton edition is especially useful because of its inclusion of Tolstoy's essays interpreting the novel according to his theories of the natural history of aggression.

A Bibliography of Human Ecology

Ardrey, Robert. *African Genesis: A Personal Investigation into the Animal Origins and Nature of Man.* New York: Atheneum, 1961.

————. *The Territorial Imperative: A Personal Inquiry into the Animal Origins of Property and Nations.* New York: Atheneum, 1966.

Barbour, Ian G. (ed.) *Western Man and Environmental Ethics.* Reading, Massachusetts and Menlo Park, California: Addison-Wesley, 1973.

Bateson, Gregory. *Steps to an Ecology of Mind.* New York: Chandler, 1972.

Bresler, Jack, ed. *Human Ecology.* Philadelphia: Addison-Wesley, 1966.

Burnet, Macfarlane. *Dominant Mammal.* New York: St. Martin's Press, 1973.

Calder, Niger. *Eden Was No Garden, An Inquiry into the Environment of Man.* New York: Holt, 1967.

Carson, Gerald. *Men, Beasts and Gods: A History of Cruelty and Kindness to Animals.* New York: Charles Scribner's Sons, 1972.

Carthy, J. D., and Ebling, F. J., eds. *The Natural History of Aggression.* New York: Academic Press, 1965.

Clark, Kenneth. *Landscape Into Art.* London: J. Murray, 1949.

Coon, Carleton. *The Hunting Peoples.* Boston: Little, Brown, 1971.

Dobzhansky, Theodosius. *Mankind Evolving.* New Haven: Yale University Press, 1962.

Dubos, René. *A God Within.* New York: Charles Scribner's Sons, 1972.

————. *Man Adapting.* New Haven: Yale University Press, 1965.

————. *So Human an Animal.* New York: Charles Scribner's Sons, 1968.

Eiseley, Loren. *The Immense Journey.* New York: Random House, 1946.

Elton, Charles S. *The Ecology of Invasions by Animals and Plants.* New York: Wiley, 1963.

Ghiselin, Michael T. "Darwin and Evolutionary Psychology," *Science* 179 (1973).

Glacken, Clarence. *Traces on a Rhodian Shore*. Berkeley: University of California Press, 1967.

Glass, David C. *Environmental Influences*. New York: Rockefeller University Press, 1968.

Gulick, Addison. "A Biological Prologue for Human Values," *Bioscience* 18:12 (1968).

Hafez, E. S. E., ed. *Behavior of Domestic Animals*. Baltimore: Williams and Wilkins, 1962.

Hardin, Garrett. *Exploring New Ethics for Survival: The Voyage of the Spaceship Beagle*. New York: Viking Press, 1972.

Huxley, Julian, ed. *Evolution as a Process*. London: Allen and Unwin, 1954.

Jewell, P. A., ed. *Play, Exploration and Territory in Mammals*. New York: Academic Press, 1966.

Lenneberg, Eric H. *The Biological Foundations of Language*. New York: Wiley, 1967.

Lorenz, Konrad. *On Aggression*. New York: Harcourt, Brace & World, 1966.

———. *Studies in Animal and Human Behavior*. 2 vols. Cambridge: Harvard University Press, 1970, 1971.

Mayr, Ernst. *Animal Species and Evolution*. Cambridge: Harvard University Press, 1963.

Morris, Desmond. *The Human Zoo*. New York: McGraw-Hill, 1969.

———, ed. *Primate Ecology*. Chicago: Aldine, 1969.

Nash, Roderick. *Wilderness and the American Mind*. New Haven: Yale University Press, 1967.

Ortega y Gassett, Jose. *The Dehumanization of Art*. New York: Doubleday, 1956.

———. *Meditations on Hunting*. Trans. Howard Wescott. New York: Charles Scribner's Sons, 1972.

Portmann, Adolph. *Animal Forms and Patterns*. New York: Schocken Books, 1967.

Read, Herbert. *Icon and Idea: The Functions of Art in the Development of Human Consciousness*. New York: Schocken Books, 1955.

Rule, Colter. "A Theory of Human Behavior Based on Studies of Non-Human Primates," *Perspectives in Biology and Medicine* 10:2 (1967).

Russell, Claire, and Russell, W. M. S. *Human Behavior, A New Approach to Human Ethology*. Boston: Little, Brown, 1961.

Schaller, George. *The Mountain Gorilla: Ecology and Behavior*. Chicago: University of Chicago Press, 1963.

Schilder, Paul. *The Image and Appearance of the Human Body*. New York: International Universities Press, 1958.

Scully, Vincent. *The Earth, the Temple and The Gods*. New Haven: Yale University Press, 1962.

Sears, Paul B. *The Ecology of Man*. Eugene: University of Oregon Press, 1957.

Sewell, Elizabeth. *The Human Metaphor*. South Bend: University of Notre Dame Press, 1964.

Shepard, Paul. *Man in the Landscape*. New York: Alfred A. Knopf, 1967.

———. *The Tender Carnivore and the Sacred Game*. New York: Charles Scribner's Sons, 1973.

Sinnott, Edmund. *The Biology of the Spirit*. New York: Macmillan, 1955.

Tejera, Victorino. *Art and Human Intelligence*. New York: Appleton-Century-Crofts, 1965.

Thomas, William L., ed. *Man's Role in Changing the Face of the Earth*. Chicago: Chicago University Press, 1956.

Thompson, D'Arcy. *On Growth and Form*. Abridged edition. London: Cambridge University Press, 1961.

Thorpe, W. H. *Learning and Instinct in Animals*. Cambridge: Harvard University Press, 1963.

Tiger, Lionel. *Men in Groups*. New York: Random House, 1969.

———, and Fox, Robin. *The Imperial Animal*. New York: Holt, 1971.

Tinbergen, Niko. *The Animal in Its World: Explorations of an Ethologist, 1932–1972*. Cambridge: Harvard University Press, 1973.

———. *The Study of Instinct*. New York: Oxford University Press, 1951.

Ucko, P. J., and Dimbleby, G. W. *The Domestication and Exploitation of Plants and Animals*. Chicago: Aldine, 1969.

Weiss, Paul A. *Within the Gates of Science and Beyond*. New York: Hafner Publishing Co., 1971.

Wheeler, Reuben. *Man, Nature and Art*. New York: Pergamon Press, 1968.

White, Lynn, Jr. "The Historical Roots of Our Ecological Crisis," *Science* 155:1203–1207 (1967).

SUGGESTED READINGS

White, Lynn, Jr. *Machina ex Deo*. Cambridge: M.I.T. Press, 1968.

Williams, George H. *Wilderness and Paradise in Christian Thought*. New York: Harper & Row, 1962.

Wynne-Edwards, V. C. *Animal Dispersion in Relation to Social Behavior*. New York: Hafner Publishing Co., 1962.

Index

Achilles (*Iliad*), 28, 49, 50–51, 71, 168

adaptation to environment: comic, 35, 39; evolutionary, 33; human, 4, 17–18; picaresque, 99–101; as creative ethic, 162

Aeschylus, 75, 76

aggression: against juveniles, 150; comic, 67–69; deterrents to, 26; ethics of, 142–144; inhibition of, 64–65; inter- and intraspecific, 64–67; legal, 76; redirection of, 64–67; social, 75–77

agriculture: ethical consequences of, 145–46; as technology, 155; *see also* domestication, farming

ambiguity, comic, 60

America, as pastoral society, 87

animality, picaresque, 112

animals of Hell (Dante's), 166

anthropocentrism, 4, 17; pastoral, 90–91; philosophical, 120; tragic 56–58

Antigone, Sophocles, 43–44, 50, 53

apocalypse, 85; sense of, 5–6; *see also* crisis

Apollo, 25

appropriate living, 188–189

Ardrey, Robert, 14

aristocracy: pastoral, 111–112; picaresque, 103–104

Aristophanes, 25–26

Aristotle, 6, 19, 23, 47, 48

art: as communication, 131–132; grotesque, 124; picaresque, 189–190; prehuman origins of, 190–191; temporal, 128; versus nature, 119; *see also* esthetics, form

artistic ecology, 134–136

artistry, picaresque, 102

atomic age, 157

Auerbach, Erich, 182

Augustine, Saint, 16

balance, esthetic and ecological, 130–134

Barth, John, 20–22

Beatrice (Dante's): 173–175; as scientist-philosopher, 176–178

beatific vision, in Dante, 178–180

beauty: animal, 121; temporal vs. spatial, 125–128; wild vs. domestic, 123–124; *see also* esthetics

Beethoven, Ludwig van, 131

behavior, comic and tragic, 21–26; *see also* ethology

behavioral sciences, weakness of, 144–145